T0294180

COSTA BLANCA MOUNTAIN ADVENTURES

THE BERNIA RIDGE AND OTHER MULTI-ACTIVITY ADVENTURES

by Mark Eddy

JUNIPER HOUSE, MURLEY MOSS,
OXENHOLME ROAD, KENDAL, CUMBRIA LA9 7RL
www.cicerone.co.uk

© Mark Eddy 2022
First edition 2022
ISBN: 978 1 78631 033 0

Printed in China on responsibly sourced paper on behalf of Latitude Press Ltd
A catalogue record for this book is available from the British Library.
All photographs are by the author unless otherwise stated.

Route mapping by Lovell Johns www.lovelljohns.com
Contains OpenStreetMap.org data © OpenStreetMap
contributors, CC-BY-SA. NASA relief data courtesy of ESRI

Updates to this guide

While every effort is made by our authors to ensure the accuracy of guide-books as they go to print, changes can occur during the lifetime of an edition. This guidebook was researched and written during the COVID-19 pandemic. While we are not aware of any significant changes to routes or facilities at the time of printing, it is likely that the current situation will give rise to more changes than would usually be expected. Any updates that we know of for this guide will be on the Cicerone website (www.cicerone. co.uk/1033/updates), so please check before planning your trip. We also advise that you check information about such things as transport, accommodation and shops locally. Even rights of way can be altered over time.

We are always grateful for information about any discrepancies between a guidebook and the facts on the ground, sent by email to updates@cicerone.co.uk or by post to Cicerone, Juniper House, Murley Moss, Oxenholme Road, Kendal, LA9 7RL.

Register your book: To sign up to receive free updates, special offers and GPX files where available, register your book at www.cicerone.co.uk.

Note on mapping

The route maps in this guide are derived from publicly available data, data-bases and crowd-sourced data. As such they have not been through the detailed checking procedures that would generally be applied to a published map from an official mapping agency. However, we have reviewed them closely in the light of local knowledge as part of the preparation of this guide.

Front cover: Nearing the end of the difficulties on the Bernia Ridge (Route 2)

CONTENTS

Acknowledgements

Many kind friends have helped shape this guide. From joining me on climbs, checking routes, preliminary proof-reading, and posing for photos. Thank you all so so much. With special thanks to:

Kate Ayres who has joined me on so many crazy adventures both in the mountains and in life. Love you.

Kim Jackson as without you we may never have even visited the Costa Blanca. Thanks for suggesting it all those years ago and for joining us every year.

Colin Uttridge for introducing me to the wonderful world of mountains, rock climbing and mountaineering. You taught me the old-school ways and I'm eternally grateful for that.

Miguel Segarra and Mila Ivars-Vaguer for being so inspiring about your local area and sharing much knowledge.

Anna Studholme for joining on many days out and being so positive.

Sam Marsland another route-checking and adventure guru. Sam would always be keen for a day with uncertainty and adventure, they came quite regularly too, thanks pal.

Mike and Ann Leese for letting us stay in your gorgeous villa in Jesús Pobre. The perfect Costa Blanca base.

Rachel Elin-Pearce and George Sanderson for looking gorgeous whilst posing for photos, but let's not forget that mega enthusiasm for all things rock and adventure and for that big day on Espolón Central.

Neil Bowmer and Ros Blackmore for route checking and feedback as well as joining me on some wild adventure days.

Andy Hedgecock for adding so many new routes in the easier – mid-grade range throughout the Costa Blanca. The bolters really are the unsung heroes of sport climbing, so here's a big shout out to you all.

Mountain safety

Every mountain walk has its dangers, and those described in this guidebook are no exception. All who walk or climb in the mountains should recognise this and take responsibility for themselves and their companions along the way. The author and publisher have made every effort to ensure that the information contained in this guide was correct when it went to press, but, except for any liability that cannot be excluded by law, they cannot accept responsibility for any loss, injury or inconvenience sustained by any person using this book.

International distress signal *(emergency only)*
Six blasts on a whistle (and flashes with a torch after dark) spaced evenly for one minute, followed by a minute's pause. Repeat until an answer is received. The response is three signals per minute followed by a minute's pause.

Helicopter rescue
The following signals are used to communicate with a helicopter:

Help needed:
raise both arms
above head to
form a 'Y'

Help not needed:
raise one arm
above head, extend
other arm downward

Emergency telephone numbers
In case of accident or emergency call 112. Ask for an English speaking operative if you require assistance with the language.

Weather reports
Spain: www.aemet.es/en/portada

Note Mountain rescue can be very expensive – be adequately insured.

Symbols used on route maps

route	ⓈS	start point
alternative/extension route	Ⓕ	finish point
glacier	ⓈⒻ	start/finish point
woodland		
urban areas	▶	route direction
regional border	>	steep ascent or descent
station/railway	>>	very steep ascent or descent
railway tunnel		
roadway tunnel		
vehicle track		
dry riverbed		
peak ▲		
church/chapel		
transmitter station		
refreshments		
cave		
campsite		
building		
col		
castle/fort		
viewpoint		
airport/helipad		
manned/unmanned refuge		
location of crag (sport climbing)		
other feature		
water feature		

Relief
in metres

1600–1800
1400–1600
1200–1400
1000–1200
800–1000
600–800
400–600
200–400
0–200

See individual maps for scale.

Symbols used on topos

———	the route	①		route numbers
	line of the route where it is not visible (through-routes etc)			notable features
		Ⓐ ↓		abseil
	approaches and descents (walking)	○		belay
- - - - -	scrambling approaches and descents that are not part of the route	Ⓔ Ⓡ		escape route
		2		grade
· · · · · · ·	alternative routes	28m		distance to ground

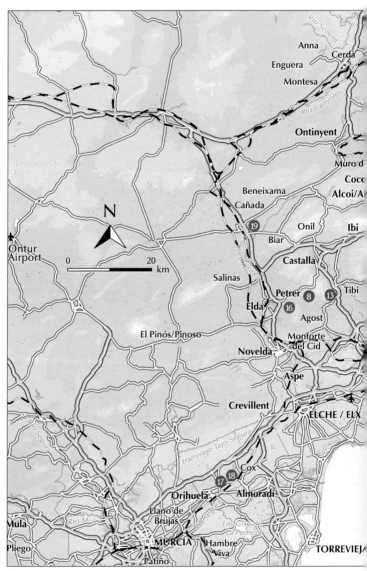

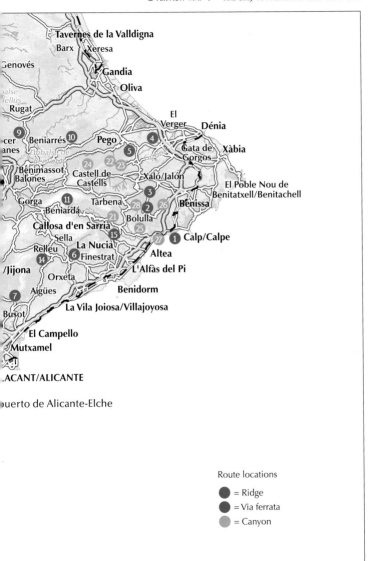

Route locations

● = Ridge
● = Via ferrata
● = Canyon

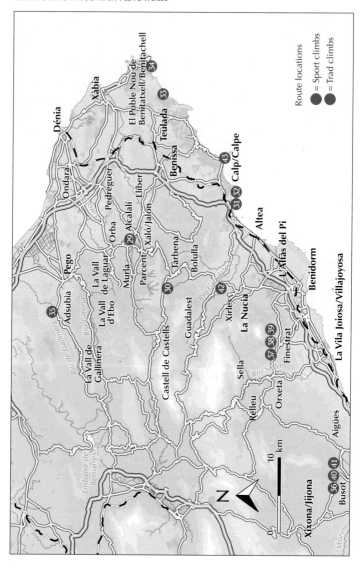

Route locations

● = Sport climbs
● = Trad climbs

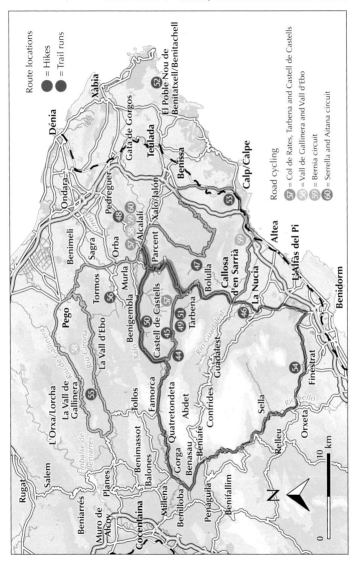

Route locations

● = Hikes
●● = Trail runs

Road cycling

57 = Col de Rates, Tarbena and Castell de Castells
58 = Vall de Gallinera and Vall d'Ebo
59 = Bernia circuit
60 = Serrella and Aitana circuit

On the early part of Benicadell (Route 9)

INTRODUCTION

The more open Barranco de Parent offers far-reaching views to Sierra Helada and the coast (Route 25)

There are parts of the world that lend themselves to outdoor adventure activities. Places like Chamonix, Banff and New Zealand come to mind. Costa Blanca is something like the winter equivalent of Chamonix. And no, not for the skiing, and yes, this is a bold claim – bear with me. Try to think of places in Europe where the rock climbing, mountaineering, road biking, canyoning and trail running are all brilliant, and most enjoyable during the winter months. Thought of any yet? Well it's all here in Costa Blanca.

A day can be spent at an easy-access, single-pitch crag; next day climb a 500m trad route; next day hit the super-smooth roads and clock up 100km on the bike; and the list just keeps on going.

Packed into a relatively small space, this karst limestone landscape is a wonderful playground, brimming with colourful flora and diverse fauna. For mountain-based fun and adventure it really is difficult to find a better winter jaunt.

This guide aims to showcase the best of the area, by offering a wide range of activities spread throughout the region and at levels to suit most.

Access to the area is quick and easy via Alicante airport. For those not wanting to fly, there are ferries

Spot the climbers! Benicadell (Route 9)

to Santander and Bilbao with just a few hours pleasant drive south once in Spain.

Once here, expect to find good motorways complemented by a well-maintained road network making in-country travel stress-free. There is a huge choice of accommodation too. Food and drink are great value, as are the eateries. Trying paella here is a must; the Valencia region is the home of paella.

Those used to going to coun-tries further afield will be pleasantly surprised by the good value offered by Costa Blanca. Saying it is 'cheap' would be to undersell the region,

although prices here are typically low. Just think of it as great value.

LANDSCAPE

The region is incredibly rocky and this almost exclusively comes in the form of sharp limestone. It's a karst landscape, where rock towers are the norm and limestone pavement is in abundance. This, along with some especially sharp vegetation can make off-path progress quite a challenge.

The mountains are typically steep, with many huge vertical faces and some are serrated. El Castellets is the longest of the serrated ridges,

The finely positioned pitch 3 on Via Pany (Route 43)

spanning several kilometres, yet still overshadowed by its mighty neighbour the Puig Campana.

PLANTS AND WILDLIFE

Once away from towns and villages there is plenty of wildlife. Ibex roam the higher mountain plateaux; and boar can be found at most heights – although you are more likely to see the evidence of their presence in the form of dug-up ground. Both species are shy and will make themselves scarce pretty quickly. If you do disturb any wildlife, be sure to give them an escape route.

Along the coast are many seabirds, including: cormorants, egrets, gulls and flamingos. Be cautious when near to gulls – they will attack for food.

If climbing on El Peñón it's not only the gulls to be cautious of. The summit area is home to an abundance of wild cats. They are only small but sharp claws and teeth can be painful, so no stopping for lunch up there.

Crag martins make their home on the crags and they often put on a spectacular display around the Toix crags.

Birds of prey include the peregrine falcon, Bonelli's eagle, and the huge griffon vulture.

Ibex on the summit plateau of Ponoch (Route 15)

Spring is the best time to enjoy wildflowers in the region. Not so wild, but worth seeing is the almond blossom. It usually flowers during February and fills the valleys with a sea of pink.

WHEN TO GO

October to April is best for mountain activities. This is when the weather cools and the summer hoards have gone home, leaving quiet roads, mountains, crags, villages and beaches. At some time between September and November the *gota fría* (cold drop) usually arrives. This is a period of unsettled weather and it can be stormy, though thankfully it usually lasts only a few days. November to mid-December tends to have the highest rainfall of winter, and this could be around eight days per month. Overall though, a winter week in Costa Blanca is likely to be sunny and warm, at around 15–20ºC.

February sees the flowering of the almond blossom, filling the valleys with pink. As this fades in March, the orange blossom arrives and fills the air with the scent of orange. March onwards is also the best time to enjoy the wildflowers.

GETTING THERE

With package tours operating in this region, flights are easy to come by and typically good value. Alicante airport has the most flight options, but it is also worth checking flights to

Almond blossom in Vall de Gallinera (Route 58)

Valencia airport. From either of these airports, the A-7 motorway provides easy access along the coast to the main accommodation and mountain areas. There is also a regular bus service from Alicante airport to Calpe.

For those not wanting to fly, there are overnight ferries to Santander and Bilbao. These are about a seven-hour drive from the region, with plenty of places of interest along the way.

Overland is possible too, with a Eurostar to Paris and connecting trains into Spain. The rail network in Spain is excellent and good value.

GETTING AROUND

Unfortunately, public transport is impractical for accessing most routes in this book, which can only be reached by car or, for some of the nearby venues, by bike.

Car hire is best arranged in advance of your visit and both airports have a wide selection of providers. Do be on your guard for any additional charges the hire companies may try to levy at collection/drop-off time. Insurance in particular can be expensive if purchased direct, so arrange this in advance. For current deals, google 'hire car excess insurance'.

ACCOMMODATION

With so many options it can be difficult to choose the best location. The coast offers most choice and generally at good rates during winter. But staying a little inland will keep journey

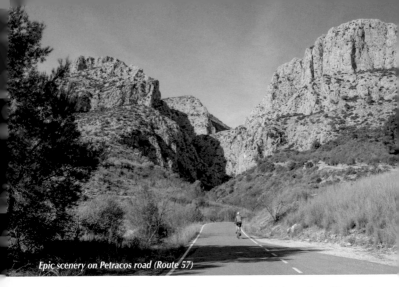
Epic scenery on Petracos road (Route 57)

times shorter and offers a more traditional experience.

There is something to suit all budgets and priorities, from basic self-catering hostels to luxury hotels and private villas. Airbnb (www.airbnb.co.uk), Booking.com (www.booking.com) and similar search sites are a good starting point.

Most accommodation is open year-round, but some of the hotels by the sea do close during winter. Good coastal bases include: Calpe, Altea, Jávea and Denia. For those seeking life away from the resorts try: Castell de Castells, Jalón, Sella, Vall de Gallinera, and Finestrat.

FOOD AND DRINK

Similar to accommodation options, the coast offers the most choice of eateries. Calle Loreto in Denia has a particularly high number of fine establishments. The Jalón valley is well served too.

Paella originated in the region of Valencia, so expect to find good examples of this most widely known Spanish dish. Lots of the seafood is locally caught, fresh and delicious.

One of the best experiences, though, is to share tapas. These small dishes can consist of almost anything, including bread, vegetables, meat, fish and rice.

Locally grown olives are served with most meals too, invariably these are delicious, but they do often arrive un-stoned, so beware of any fragile teeth.

LANGUAGE

Valenciano and Castellano (Valencian and Castilian) are both widely spoken.

To confuse matters, they are also often mixed to create dialects. A phrase book or app will be useful for non-Spanish speakers, although many locals speak and understand enough English to manage. Along the coast most people do speak English, but inland and in the small mountain villages expect to have the phrase book out a lot more. A few words can go a long way.

It is normal to see names on signposts crossed out. This will be the Castilian name, as some Valencians want independence from Madrid. For a glossary of some terms you might come across, see Appendix C.

Calle Loreta in Denia is home to many excellent eateries and exudes a fine atmosphere

Big air abseils in the Barranco del Pas de Tancat (Route 21)

MAPS

In recent years the quality of mapping has improved and now a wide selection of maps is available.

The best overall map of the area, with good detail at 1:40,000 scale and in a clear format, is *Costa Blanca Mountains*, published by Discovery Walking Guides Ltd and available online. It also has the advantage of being fully waterproof and extremely durable.

For more detail at 1:20,000 scale are the *Terra Ferma* maps published by Editorial Piolet. These are available locally in bookshops, outdoor gear shops and even some fuel stations.

For the Serrella mountain range, the most detailed map is the *La Serrella* (1:20,000 scale), published by El Tossal. This is also available locally.

Making the short abseil from Forada ridge (Route 8)

The Editorial Piolet and El Tossal maps are printed on thin, flimsy paper that does not stand up well to usage, a map case is worth bringing if you can.

WAYMARKING AND ACCESS

There are markings to show whenever you are on an official trail. They are usually painted on rock or trees in yellow and white but may also be green and white or red and white. At turnings, these markings will be curved in the direction of travel. If a cross is painted, this is showing the wrong way. But please note that some of the routes described in this guide do venture off main paths onto climbing/ scrambling terrain – so if in doubt, follow the route description and not the paint markings, as these are showing walking routes.

HEALTH AND SAFETY

Although the coastal resorts are bustling places, the mountains here are very quiet. On many routes in this guide you are unlikely to see another person all day. If travelling alone it would be prudent to let someone know of your intended route each day and an expected return time. Or better still, convince a friend to join you.

We have never come across dangerous animals while in the mountains, although territorial dogs can sometimes be a nuisance. A variety of snakes are present in the region,

Many of the lower trails on Olta are well signposted (Route 53)

some being venomous, so it's best to give them a wide berth. In fact, they normally scuttle away into the undergrowth, always eager to make their escape.

The processional caterpillar is worth a mention. It builds silky web nests in young pine trees and drop onto the ground during springtime to form a long line of caterpillars. Do not touch them, their hairs are an extreme irritant.

You may come across the sign 'Abejas' (Bees). This is to warn of nearby beehives. They will generally be busy around the hives, simply keeping a little distance should be enough to avoid harm.

The weather is usually very settled. But when is does rain, it can be

on an epic scale, with dry riverbeds quickly turning into angry torrents of impassable water. Limestone is slippery when wet and the trails soon become sludge-like, making progress both difficult and unpleasant. So, in the unlikely event of poor weather, consider having a rest day, town day or visit another area day. And keep it in mind that, when the rain does fall in Spain, you should stay away from the mountains.

Insurance

For all UK citizens it is a good idea to obtain a GHIC card (these are free via the NHS website); EU citizens can apply for a free EHIC card. This give access to the same emergency healthcare that a local would receive, at the same cost. However, it does not cover repatriation to your home country, nor does it cover ongoing medical costs or other losses, so travel insurance is still essential. Make sure that your policy covers the activities you plan to undertake to avoid any unpleasant (and expensive!) surprises. Current providers include:

- True Traveller offers easy-to-tailor policies that cover adventurous activities, as well as regular travel insurance such as lost/stolen luggage, www.truetraveller.com
- The British Mountaineering Council is, for many, the 'go-to' place for rock-climbing/ adventure sports policies, www.thebmc.com
- Snowcard offers easy-to-tailor policies for the adventure traveller, www.snowcard.co.uk.

USING THIS GUIDE

The aim of this guide is to provide an introduction to the wide variety of activities the Costa Blanca has to offer. As it is such a large region, this is really a 'highlights of' the Costa Blanca.

Costa Blanca is a fantastic destination for outdoor enthusiasts looking to extend their 'summer' activities into the winter months. It is the perfect antidote to a UK winter.

This guide has been conveniently divided into activity sections, with detailed descriptions at the start of each chapter. Activities covered in this guide are:
- Ridge scrambles and climbs
- Via ferratas
- Canyoning
- Sport climbing
- Trad climbing

Traversing on Castillo Salvatierra (Route 19)

- Hiking
- Trail running
- Road cycling

The first pitch of Scorpion (Route 42)

A summary of activities can be found in Appendix A. Appendix B contains a list of useful contacts.

Activities

Each route/activity will include a box providing some summary details.

A 'what3words' address is offered to help you locate the start point. What3words has allocated every 3m x 3m square in the world a unique three-word address. These addresses won't change. The what3words addresses are indicated by /// and displayed next to the start point in the information box. Download the what-3words app onto your smartphone, type or scan the three-word address, and you can use Google maps on your phone to get you to the correct location. There are also notes on how to access the start point.

All activities have been graded and further details of the systems used can be found in the introduction for each chapter. Estimated timings are also offered where applicable but do be aware these are subjective. Height gain and distance have also been included where applicable as this will be of further aid in estimating the time required to complete a route.

Throughout the route description, features that appear on the accompanying maps and photo topos are highlighted in **bold** to aid navigation.

RIDGES

Maigmó ridge (Route 13)

🕊 RIDGES

Big views from the Ferrer Ridge (Route 3)

Costa Blanca is one of the most mountainous regions on the Iberian Peninsula. With this come many wonderfully serrated ridges. At first glance they can seem difficult to access. But not so: the small and well-surfaced mountain roads here allow much height to be gained the easy way.

Many visitors are here for the world-famous sport climbing and may at most tackle one ridge during a visit, on a 'rest day'. Those looking for a more mountaineering style of adventure will be aiming to traverse a few of these lesser-known gems. Any of these days out will leave a lasting impression.

The more popular routes are semi-equipped with bolts at crux and abseil stations. The more esoteric offerings away from the coast will have almost no fixed gear and will require a light trad climbing rack. Go prepared for a mountain day, pack some warmer layers and be sure to carry a head torch. Bright sunshine at 5pm turns to darkness by 6pm during the winter months.

Treat the rock with more caution than on clip-up crags. Fewer people make the effort to traverse these ridges, so loose rock isn't just a possibility, it's an integral part of the adventure.

Grading

Routes in this section have been graded according to UIAA climbing grades (supplemented with standard UK scrambling grades where necessary), with the exception of Route 12, which has been assigned a French sport-climbing grade since it is fully bolted. See Appendix E for a comparison table of climbing grades.

ROUTE 1

Toix Ridge Integral (Este y Oeste)

Start point	Mirador above Maryvilla (Calpe) ///bribery.pillow.diplomas
Grade	IV
Time	Total time 5–6hr: approach 40min; Espolón Arta 2hr; walking time from the Mirador to Toix Oeste/Placa 20min; Toix Oeste 2hr; return 20min
Length	510m plus scrambling/walking
Aspect/conditions	Toix Este has sun until early afternoon, while Toix Oeste and the ridge above receives sun from mid-morning until sunset. All sections of these crags can be windy, and especially so along the ridges.
Equipment	60m rope, 10 quickdraws, 4 alpine 'draws, 4 120cm-slings, and a light rack

This route visits two entirely different sections of the Sierra de Toix range.

Toix Este is a rambling rocky buttress perched high above the sea and overlooking Calpe and El Peñón de Ifach. A number of routes lead to the top of this crag, and for this itinerary we choose Espolón Arta.

Toix Oeste and Placa Upper, where the remaining section of ridge lies, is a larger and steeper crag with a huge variety of climbing. Our chosen line here is immediately left of route 'Alistair', but this route works equally well, as do any of the routes further left. There is much scope for variation. The crags of Toix are popular and can be busy at weekends but the ridge is usually quiet.

Access and parking

Turn off the N-332 into the *urbanización* Maryvilla, which lies between Calpe and Altea. Follow the brown/pink signs through the *urbanización* until you reach the Mirador. Park at a small lay-by at the end of the road and next to a barrier.

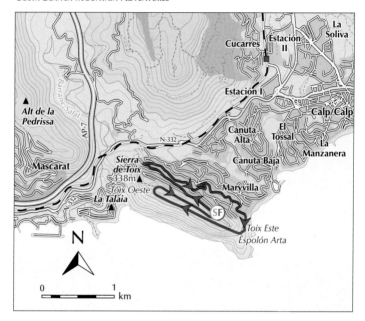

Approach

Walk back along the road going downhill, keeping right at a fork then sharp right at an N-332 sign. Then turn sharp left at the 'no through road' sign and the large bins, to soon go sharp right past more bins, still heading downhill.

Go right at a T-junction and pass a row of garages. Bear left at the next fork to go downhill and reach a 'stop' sign. Turn left here, continuing downhill to another 'stop', and turn right here. Go right again at the next 'stop' sign and onto a 'no through road'. At the end of the road, go over a chain to continue along a track that soon bears right under crags perched high above the sea.

At a promontory, where there is red writing on the rock (route information), take the small track leading towards the crag. **Espolón Arta** starts at a left-to-right rib at the base of an orange and grey hollow.

The ridge

The first part of this route uses sport climbing grades as this section is fully equipped. The second part of the route uses UIAA climbing grades.

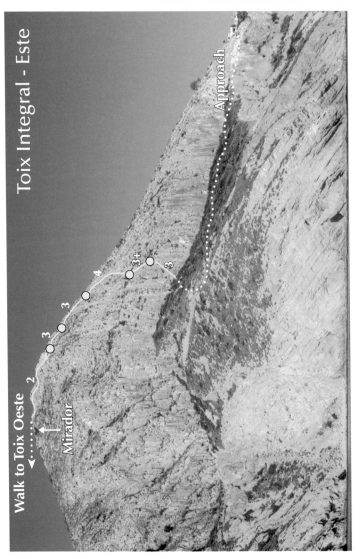

Toix Integral - Este

Approach

Walk to Toix Oeste

Mirador

2

3

3

3

4

3+

3

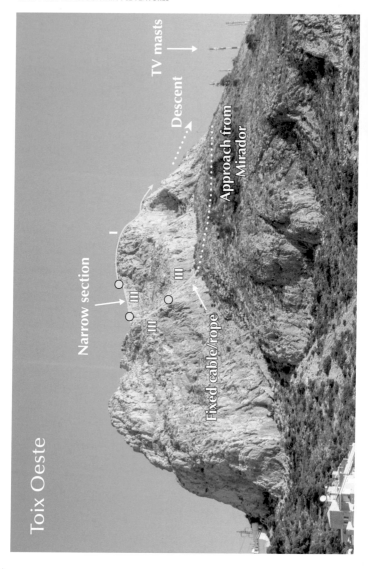

Toix Oeste

Narrow section

TV masts

Descent

Approach from Mirador

Fixed cable/rope

1) 3, 25m Start where 'Espolón Arta' is painted on the rock. Follow the right-trending rib with threads to a bolted belay.

2) 3+, 30m Continue more directly, following threads and bolts, to a belay station. Belay here or continue a couple of metres onto the huge ledge with single-bolt belay backed up with threads.

3) 4, 40m Faint white arrows lead the way up and right to a fine slab. Climb this, aiming for the skyline, and follow it until you reach a bolt and thread belay on the rib.

4) 3, 33m Follow the vegetated rib more easily, and after 30m bear slightly left until you reach a niche with spike belay.

5) 3, 30m Descend leftwards passing a bolted belay and from here trend upwards following arrows and occasional bolts to reach a large clearing. There is a single-bolt belay by a red blob at the back of this ledge.

The following section is about 200m long and mostly grade 1 scrambling.

Go leftwards (looking inland) across the wide clearing to reach slabs shelving up. Follow these rightwards to a corner and gain the crest here. Stay on the crest as it narrows on its way to the Mirador (viewpoint).

From the **Mirador** follow the wide track around a sharp corner to reach the south/Benidorm side of the headland, and follow this to the **TV masts** and the end of the good track. A path continues in the same direction, descending under crags. Paint-blobs and cairns occasionally mark the way. Pass under a big orange wall of recessed rock before reaching grey slabs with a fixed rope to the left side and above the name **'Alistair'**.

6) III, 35m Follow the fixed rope until you reach a level section with cable leading left and rope leading right. Belay here at the red blob.

7) III+, 50m From here take a direct line up broken grey slabs keeping right of the steep yellow wall. Trend slight right until just below the ridge and belay.

8) III+, 65m Follow the spectacular ridge which is straightforward but very exposed. As the ridge begins to widen there are plentiful spike belays. It is easy to split this long pitch into two shorter pitches with an intermediate belay halfway along the ridge at a small, grassy stance on the left.

Gain the summit and easier, but no less dramatic, terrain. Grade I scrambling remains as the ridge forges towards the TV masts.

Return
Follow the wide track back along the headland.

ROUTE 2

Bernia Ridge

Start point	Parking area near Bernia Restaurant/Casas de Bernia, CV-749, Jalón, ///persuade.piazzas.doves
Grade	IV
Time	Total time 6–7hr: approach 1hr; ridge 4hr 30min; descent 45min. If including the main summit add 2hr to the total time.
Length	Approximately 3km
Aspect/conditions	No shelter and sun all day
Equipment	35m rope (minimum), helmet, harness, belay device, prussic cord, 10 quickdraws, rock shoes (optional)
Abseils	The route involves a 20m abseil; other shorter abseils are optional.

The most striking and recognisable skyline in the region. This is an absolute classic. Once seen, any mountaineer will be drawn in by the seemingly endless serrated rocky towers, for a mountaineering day out that shouldn't be under-estimated. The ridge hovers around the 1000m contour for much of its length and can be exposed to inclement weather, high winds and intense sun. So check the forecast and go prepared. Once on the ridge there is no water and no easy way off.

Access and parking

From the N-332 follow signs for Xaló/Jalón and immediately turn left onto the CV-749 Pinós and follow this to its end at a T-junction. Turn left and park shortly after the Bernia Restaurant.

Approach

From the parking area follow a good track heading for the seaward end of the ridge. After about 15 minutes you'll reach a *font* (natural spring), then climb the steps through rocky outcrops leading onto a smaller path. Keep on this path as it climbs steadily uphill to reach the **forat** (a large natural hole through the base of

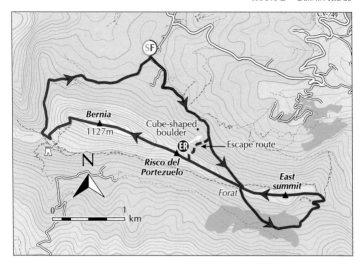

the ridge). Crawl through the tunnel and, once on the south side, turn left towards Font de Rostoll. Follow a small but good track for 400m (seven minutes).

Pass through a clump of holm oak and turn off this path. Continue for another 500m on vague tracks and then take an ascending traverse line to reach the start of the ridge, after about 10–15 minutes of walking through scrub terrain.

The ridge

Once on the ridge the route is clear for most of the way, and occasionally marked with red paint. Many variations exist but sticking with the red dots and arrows ensures an easier passage. Stay on the crest for maximum fun – this gives some airy positions at about grade I. Upon reaching a bolted belay at a notch, a short abseil can be set up to descend this (10m), or down-climb at grade I. Soon you reach another bolted belay for a short abseil into an exposed position; this too can be down-climbed with care at about grade I. Follow a descending traverse line along a groove to reach easier ground and a col. **Note:** this is where the shorter variation joins (see below).

More grade I scrambling follows, and is now mostly on the north side of the ridge so beware of any lingering dampness.

You will reach a bolted belay, which can either be abseiled to a ledge (circa 10m) or you can rope up and climb straight across the narrow ridge direct for full effect (bolts protect both options). There is a single-bolt belay on the far side.

Bernia ridge – north side

Descent from summit to Fort

Descent from col after technical section

Approach

Cube boulder

Three prominent fins

Starting col accessed from north side

East Peak

Quick start

ER

II/III

4+

II/III

I

From now on the ridge is narrow and extremely exposed, but not technically difficult. After a short down-climb you'll reach a bolted abseil station. This abseil is 20m to the wide and flat ledge, or 17m to sloping platforms. From here easy scrambling over pleasant slabs regains the undulating and widening ridge. Ahead are **three prominent fins**, with the right-hand fin giving a fantastic 4+ (fully bolted) climbing section. To reach this, descend broken ground right, then leftwards, before a tricky traverse leads back right. Soon a short walk leads between the fins. This area is a good place to stop for lunch as it will provide shelter from the sun and wind.

The climb is very well bolted and can easily be aided if required. 10 quickdraws will be sufficient. The initial moves are the most challenging. Once hands are on top of the fin things ease somewhat. Be sure to peer over the other side!

The bolted belay above is on a good but exposed ledge. More exposed scrambling leads directly up to a minor summit. Continue to weave across the ridge to reach another abseil station at the top of a broad chimney. Avoid this by scrambling rightwards (looking down). A number of false summits keep coming before descending on the north side to a col complete with **log book**. A few metres beyond the log book is a bolted abseil station. About 15m further and you'll reach easy ground below, or simply scramble to the easy ground at about UIAA grade I. This is the top of the big scree run used as a descent. 'Ski' down this to reach the main path back to the parking area (a path exists just to the right of the scree slope and is easier) or continue to the main summit via further UIAA grade I scrambling and walking. The continuation route heads across the top of the scree run to reach in-situ cord marking the start of the continuation. This leads to the main summit of Bernia and is worthwhile, albeit considerably easier than previous sections.

Descent

From the log book col either abseil from the bolted abseil station or down-climb about 15m to reach easy ground. Keep descending northwards onto the big scree run, staying to the right of the huge cube-shaped boulder far below. Once you reach the main walkers' path, turn left for an easy walk back to the car and hopefully coffee and cake in the restaurant.

For those not wishing to tackle the scree slopes, keep to the extreme right (looking down) to find a small path weaving through the rocky ground.

Descent from the main Bernia summit

For those wanting to tick the main summit after completing the technical ridge section, continue for about 1.5km along the now wider ridge, taking the line of least resistance. This is never more than grade I scrambling. From the summit, waymarkers lead southwards down to the **fort**. Follow these on a rocky path all

Bernia ridge - south side approach detail

Continuation scramble/climb along main ridge ....

Equipped abseils or down-climb at Grade 2 →

Grade 1 continuation to summit ....

Forat/tunnel from north

Log book col on north side

Nearing the end of the difficulties on the Bernia ridge

the way to the fort, then turn right on an excellent path that leads around the western end of the ridge, and this leads back to the parking area.

Shorter variation
If short on time, or wanting an easier day, this slightly shorter trip encapsulates the atmosphere and all the best bits of the ridge.

Upon reaching the *forat*, don't go through this, but instead scramble leftwards, following green paint blobs from just left of the *forat*. The scrambling soon eases at a small path leading up to reach the ridge at the col that would be reached after the second abseil if you were completing the full traverse (see above).

ROUTE 3
Sierra Ferrer Ridge

Start point	Verd I Vent/Casa Susi restaurants, CV-749 (Bernia), /// injunction.gnats.cackling
Grade	I
Time	Total time 3–4hr: approach 1hr; route 1hr 30min; return 45min
Length	750m
Aspect/conditions	Sun all day, exposed to any wind
Equipment	No technical equipment required

This, the easiest of the ridges featured in this guide, offers really fun scrambling at an amenable level. The ridge is best viewed from Col de Rates on the road between Parcent and Tarbena. It gives a formidable and impenetrable feel, with seemingly difficult access. Thankfully, access is straightforward and one can surmount this magnificent ridge with fairly little effort. In terms of difficulty, it's only just a grade I scramble, so it's similar to Striding Edge in the English Lake District.

Being doable in around three hours, this makes a good 'rest day' from the longer ridges or other mountain adventures. Mid to late afternoon is best, when the sun dips low in the sky to give dramatic light over the surrounding mountains.

Access and parking

From the town of Jalón/Xaló, follow the CV-749 towards Bernia and Masserof. Park in a lay-by on this road next to the Verd I Vent/Casa Susi restaurants.

Approach

Opposite the **Verd I Vent** restaurant is a broad track, follow this for about 100m to a wooden post showing a mountain bike route (BTT). Turn right here, just before the track goes uphill. A good path traverses through scrub before descending into a shallow valley. Turn left here at another mountain biking sign and shortly after you reach a surfaced lane – 10 minutes from the start.

Turn right onto the lane, initially going downhill, and passing terraces on either side to reach **Caserío del Mirador** (with big solar panels). Go left here at the 'Les Murtes' sign to continue uphill. About 15 minutes from the start to here.

Soon a left fork leads up to the **Donkey Sanctuary**. Keep right until the next sharp turning and, as the road sweeps back around rightwards, take a small path on the left. This traverses through pine woods above a wide gully to the right. Follow this path as it ascends the narrowing rocky gully to reach a levelling shortly before a house and olive terraces. Turn left here onto a small path marked by cairns, keeping the house to your right.

A little overgrown at first, the path improves as it makes its way uphill, initially through more pine woodland. Once clear of the woods, aim for the rocky ground above, always keeping to the path, which is marked with occasional red paint and cairns. Go around the left end of the ridge to begin the scramble on the eastern side (one hour from the start).

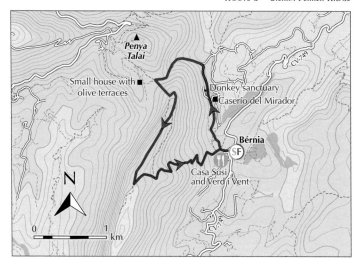

The ridge

Red paint marks the start and three bolts have been placed at about 5m intervals on this initial section. Although there appears to be no need for them, they are a convenient marker for the start.

Initially the ridge provides easy scrambling mixed with exposed walking up to and passing a large antenna. Beyond this, the crest narrows. There is an occasional track on the right-hand side for those not wanting full exposure the whole way.

A short and very **narrow section** awaits. This is about 40–50m of very airy but straightforward scrambling before the ridge returns to wider terrain as it gains a little height before descending to a **rocky col**.

From here stay left of the ridge for 30m until a clamber up regains the now-wide crest. Then aim for a lone pine on an improving path, mostly on the right side of the crest, until you reach a **shallow col**. Cross to the left side then back right heading towards a large pine tree, and continue on the right side towards a **large pinnacle** by another pine about 150m further on.

Cross to the left side here and follow the narrow path as it traverses under the crest and slightly downhill to reach a broad track in the pine woods.

Descent

Once on this good path, follow it downhill back to the road at **Verd I Vent**.

Ferrer ridge

Narrow section
40 - 50m

Rocky
col

Shallow
col

Large pinnacle

Descent

Approach

ROUTE 4
Segaria Ridge

Start point	Segaria parking area, Partida Vinyals, Beniarbeig, ///rigid. hyphens.paperwork
Grade	Section 1: IV+; Section 2: I; Section 3: III
Time	Section 1: 5–6hr; Section 2: 3hr; Section 3: 4hr. Allow about 10hr for a full traverse.
Length	4km over 3 sections
Aspect/conditions	Sun all day, exposed to the wind
Equipment	50m rope (minimum), helmet, harness, belay device, prussic cord. A selection of slings, medium cams and nuts to protect the climbing pitches.
Abseils	Maximum length of 25m

Rising abruptly from the coastal plain, the huge crest of Segaria will grab and hold the attention of anyone lucky enough to lay eyes on it. It's around 4km long and with numerous technical sections. We split the ridge into three manageable sections: all are enjoyable independently (using the escape routes marked on the map and topo), or for a grandiose day out can be linked for a full traverse.

Access and parking

From the N-332 just north of Ondara take the turning for Benidoleig. Go straight over the first roundabout, then left at the second roundabout, and immediately left again at the third roundabout heading towards Sagra and Beniarbeig.

Take the second right onto Partida Vinyals, following a sign for Segaria Parc. The parking area is about 2km along this road and on the right.

From the parking area, footpaths go in all directions.

Approaches
Section 1: For the eastern (seaward) section take a track through long grass and scrub, heading east with the ridge on the left. After 10 minutes you'll reach an

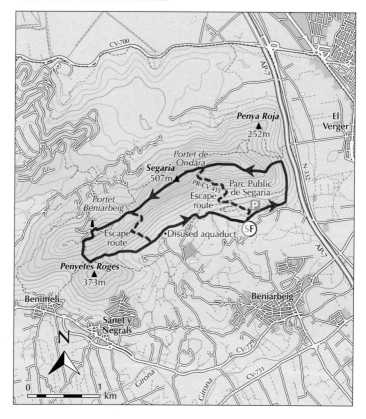

old building with a tower. On the corner of the building are yellow and white waymarkings. Follow these as they lead, rather vague at times, onto a narrow path towards the seaward end of the ridge. Continue under and beyond the nose of the ridge until you reach broken ground and vague tracks lead up and to the left.

Section 2: For the easier middle section take the PR-CV 415 to **Parc Public de Segaria** and continue up towards Portet de Ondara. This is the notch up and slightly left when viewed from the parking area.

A good track leads past holiday cottages, then follow signs for the 'Mirador' on a waymarked path uphill, leading to a disused aqueduct. Portet de Ondara is clearer from here and signed going uphill on a vague path which zigzags up

45

towards large crags to the right of the vegetated notch in the ridge. Walk under these to gain the notch.

Section 3: For the final section of ridge, it is the very prominent notch much further left that must be gained. This is **Portet Beniarbeig**. Gain the **aqueduct** as described in the Section 2 approach above and follow this westward towards Cova de Bolumni. At the sign for Racons straight ahead and Bolumni to the right, go right and uphill towards the Bolumni cave. This path zigzags up all the way to the big notch of **Portet de Ondara**.

Section 1

The vague path soon disappears, but continue scrambling upwards, following the occasional cairn. After around 10 minutes of scrambling through a mixture of bushes, scrub and rocks the terrain on the left eases a little to allow a more amenable passage. Follow the line of least resistance leftwards until you reach a level area by an impressive terrace. If not geared up already, this is a good place to do so.

Traverse leftwards on easy slabs to reach a notch and double-bolt belay. From here, follow the crest of the ridge, passing a bolted belay after 60m.

These initial pitches are no more than grade III/IV.

Soon the ridge narrows into a fine arête, straightforward and magnificently exposed, and soon after that you'll reach a bolted abseil station. It is a **diagonal abseil** of 20m to the notch, or 25m straight down into the gully. Going for the notch is slightly easier overall. Climb out of the notch directly on fine slabs leading to more narrow sections and a detached pinnacle. An airy step onto the right side of this allows an amenable crossing. The ridge drops down slightly into another notch with much steeper ground ahead. Traverse ledges leftwards until a scoop can be gained which leads back rightwards at about grade V. There may be some threads in places helping to show the way. Continue on slabs trending rightwards to reach easier ground and a thread belay below a large ledge. From here the summit cross can be seen and is easily gained. A final narrow and exposed section of about 30m follows before the ridge begins to merge with the wider hillside. Stay on the high ground, following the occasional cairn to reach the col of **Portet de Ondara**.

Section 2

From the col of **Portet de Ondara** turn left (west) to follow the broad ridge through scrub and occasionally dense vegetation. Yellow and white paint marks the route. The summit trig is reached after about 25 minutes. There may be a log book here. The ridge continues in an undulating fashion, without the help of waymarking. Stay on the higher ground for most interest. Simply pick a route over the rocky ground to best avoid any spiky bushes – they bite!

Scramblers nearing the end of the ridge

You will reach a gap in the ridge that is best negotiated via a vegetated gully on the left.

Exit the gap on the left and traverse across slabs until easier scrambling back rightwards regains the broad crest. Pick a rocky line over high ground until just before the huge notch. About 30m before the notch is a narrow gap on the right (north). Scramble down this on the north side to enter the notch of **Portet Beniarbeig**. This is by far the easiest part of the ridge and suitable for adventurous walkers with a head for heights.

Section 3

Drop down a few metres on the south side of the notch and scramble leftwards to a rising ramp; follow this back right to reach a short arête leading to a spacious ledge with a tree.

Follow slabs behind the tree before trending right to reach the ridge proper. This soon narrows spectacularly. Stay on the crest for the full experience.

Descend to a small notch via rocks on the left, then cross to the north side of the ridge passing through the notch. Easy slabs regain the crest. Look out for a small cave (Bolumni) on the left at a wide section. Stay slightly right to regain the crest and follow this. It soon descends to a short gully on the right with a flake at its top. Descend this (tricky) for about 5m to reach an old cable-belay station. Go over vegetated terrain towards the antennae until you reach a pinnacle by a narrow gully. Descend this on the south side for 5m (possible tat in situ on the left that could be backed up for an abseil), then traverse left (looking in) to bushes and a bolted **abseil** station. 22m reaches the ground.

Escape options
There are two very prominent notches along the ridge – Portet de Ondara and Portet Beniarbeig, both being easy places to escape the ridge. Escape from anywhere else along the ridge will prove difficult and spiky.

Descent
Reverse the approach descriptions for each section (see Approaches, above). For the final section walk to the antennae and from there follow tracks left (south side of the ridge), either to descend to the road, or to follow the disused aqueduct back to the recreation area.

 ROUTE 5

Cresta del Migdia

Start point	Tormos cemetery, ///resurgent.clambered.boringly
Grade	II
Time	Total time 4hr: approach 30min; route 2hr 30min; return 1hr
Length	750m
Aspect/conditions	Sun all day. Exposed to the wind
Equipment	30m rope

With the long and sinuous Segaria ridge so close by, it would be easy to overlook this little gem. But, when viewed from the Orba valley, the curving arête stands proud and begs to be explored. Easy access from the coast, good approach paths and sensational positions, all at such an amenable grade, make this a 'go-to' objective for the mid-grade scrambler. The rock is of very good quality, sharp and solid for much of the route, making progress a real pleasure.

Access and parking

From the N-332 follow signs for Pedreguer and go through this town. At a roundabout by a car workshop turn onto the CV-720 towards Alcalalí, then take the second turning on the right onto the CV-733 to Benidoleig. Go through this village and join the CV-731 to Orba. At the T-junction in Orba, turn right onto the CV-715 to Tormos. Once in Tormos follow signs for the cemetery which is above the village on its western side. Park here.

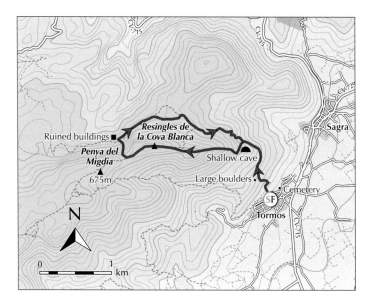

Approach

Continue on foot on the trail marked PR-CV 58 Ebo–Pego Figuereta. The path weaves through some **impressive boulders**; no doubt these could provide endless hours of fun, too. At a junction marked by a fluorescent dot, follow the right-hand branch traversing easily through light pine woodland. About 150m further on, look out for a fork in the path, marked by green and white paint. Take the left fork ascending gently, and soon you'll come to a cairn and green paint blob marking an exit from the main path. Go left at the cairn and follow a vague path over uneven terrain, aiming just left of a **cave at the base of the ridge**. About 30m left

49

of the cave, and in a groove, is another blob of green paint. This marks the start
of the scramble.

The ridge

Climb up to the green blob and follow slabs rightwards from this, keeping to the
cleanest rocks. You will soon gain the ridge proper. Views now open up and the
crest narrows; stick to the crest for most fun. At a steep orange buttress, go left
(marked by green and red paint) and ascend pleasant grey slabs back onto the
crest which opens out ahead once more. When you reach an orange scar below
a huge flake, climb this just left of the scar to gain splendid positions on the
ridge. A long easy section now lies ahead. There is plenty of scope for variation,
with escapes to the left never far away. A brief gap in the ridge allows for more
dynamic movement – jump over this to continue along the crest (or by-pass on the
left), passing the occasional green blob. When the ridge comes to its sudden end,
go slightly left, following the green paint, to descend slabs to a col.

Descent

From the col drop down on the north side and pick a route over this rough terrain.
There are small cairns, but these are difficult to spot and follow. Set a course for
the **ruined buildings** at the lower col and aim to reach these, with some bush-
whacking. Wearing long trousers will be most helpful for this section. Once close
to the ruins, you'll find a PR walking route. Follow this improving path as it traverses back under the north face of the ridge. At a junction follow signs for **Tormos**
to arrive back at the start.

ROUTE 6
El Realet/Alt del Castellet

Start point	Parking between Finestrat and Sella, CV-758, ///retiring. dwarfism.airlock
Grade	IV+
Time	Total time 6–7hr: approach 40min; route 5hr; return 45min (with vehicles at either end)
Length	1km
Aspect/conditions	Sunny. Exposed to wind
Equipment	60m rope, light trad rack with plenty of 120cm slings, and some medium cams
Abseils	The route involves four abseils of 30m, 25m, 25m and 10m

Taken as a whole, this is by far the longest ridge in the region, by quite a margin. It is also one of the narrowest and most spectacular. To complete a full traverse is a multi-day outing and beyond the scope of this book. There is a locally produced guidebook describing the complete traverse over six days!

The section described here is known as 'El Realet' or 'Alt del Castellet' and takes in the three summits at the eastern end of the ridge. This makes for a fantastic and exciting day out with a proper mountaineering feel. Escape options are limited, shade and shelter are virtually non-existent, so go prepared.

As the majority of the ridge is a traverse, all members of the party need to feel comfortable on about UK Severe grade terrain. The climbing is never particularly difficult, but the exposure and often spaced protection certainly add a grade.

Access and parking

There are two options here, and whether you have access to just one vehicle, or to two, will determine which is best for you.

Single-car option/parking point A: From Finestrat take the CV-758 towards Sella, follow this until the 12km marker and shortly after this is a turning on the right. Park here near the chain barrier.

Two-car option/parking points A and B: Organising two vehicles for this can seem like a bit of a hassle, but it pays off, with less time spent on foot on the tarmac. One car needs to be left at the 'Pick-up point' at the end of the ridge. This can be found by following the CV-758 out of Finestrat going towards Sella. After 1.2km and opposite 'Villa Sol', turn right by post boxes and bins. Keep on this narrow road until you get to the sign for 'Finca Cajubama, El Realet NR.72'. Bear slight left here and continue for about 1km to a small lay-by and parking among pine trees. Leave one car here and return to the main road going towards Sella and follow this to just after the 12km sign. Turn right here and park by the chain barrier.

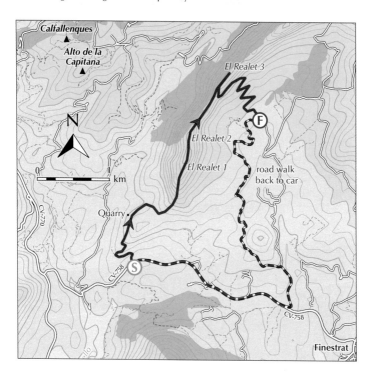

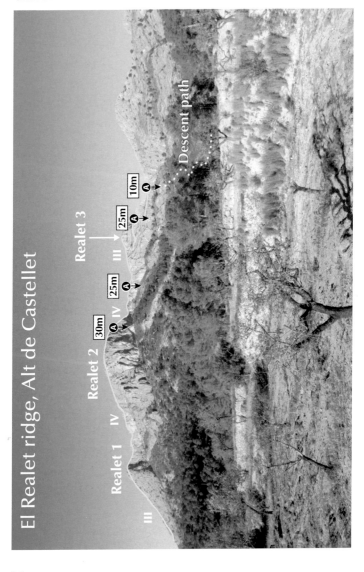

El Realet ridge, Alt de Castellet

Realet 1

Realet 2

Realet 3

III

IV

30m

25m

25m

10m

Descent path

One of the many super-exposed sections of El Realet

Approach

From parking point 'A', walk along the minor lane uphill towards a quarry. Just before a barrier, turn right onto a rougher dirt track and follow this, passing the **quarry** on your left and below. At a bend in the track turn right (about 20 minutes from the start) bear right up to another col at a bend in the track. From here go left to follow a vague path leading uphill through pine then scrub to reach the ridge.

The ridge

Start at a red blob and arrow next to a large bush. Scramble past the red paint to find a fine arête presenting itself. Follow more occasional red paint spots, staying on the crest and in increasingly wonderful situations all the way to the first summit of **El Realet 1**.

Locate the bolted belay and down-climb (IV) to gain the serrated ridge in sensational positions. Continue along this with occasional bolts and easier climbing/scrambling to gain **El Realet 2**. From here an easy descent reaches a bolted abseil station above the steep ground. **Abseil 30m** to sloping ledges. Scramble over to a small col before continuing along the castellated ridge, equipped with the occasional bolt. Just after a tricky step you'll reach another bolted stance. **Abseil 25m** (on left/south side) to reach easy ground. From here walk up to the summit of **El Realet 3**.

Retrace your steps for around 70m to a small notch in the ridge, go through this and onto a vague path traversing ledges under the summit/ridge. Occasional cairns mark the way to a notch by a pine tree. Locate an abseil station and **abseil 25m** to ledges. Continue traversing left (looking out), and after about 50m you'll reasch another **abseil station** at a V-notch. 10m reaches the descent path.

Descent

Vague paths descend leftwards under the craggy ridge, keep to these following the occasional cairn. A shallow valley below is your target and a variety of small and indistinct paths lead there. Once in the valley, walk around the almond terraces on their right side. Soon after, take a small path that leads up to the higher ground on the right and follow this as it trends left to reach the road at the parking area. If you only brought one vehicle, walk back along the road to the start point (see map).

🕇 ROUTE 7

Cresta del Canelobre, Cabezón de Oro

Start point	Cueves de Canelobre parking area, Busot, ///leers.depict. raspberry
Grade	III
Time	Total time 2hr 20min: approach 5min; route 2hr; return 15min
Length	40m via ferrata, 155m climb/scrambling
Aspect/conditions	Sun all day, exposed to the wind
Equipment	60m rope minimum, a few alpine quickdraws, slings, a light trad rack
Abseils	The route involves three abseils of 30m, 20m and 20m

Occasional visitors often overlook this mountain, but the locals are aware of its fine attributes. When viewed from the A-7 motorway it looks like a big boring lump of spiky scrub. Once on the Busot road, the true scale of the mountain begins to be revealed, and the amount of rock is huge. Many equipped sport-climbing sectors are already developed and no doubt more are on the way.

This route tackles the striking ridgeline directly above the parking area at Cuevas de Canelobre. Since being equipped with a via ferrata (suitable for children), and abseil stations for the descent, this ridge has become a multi-activity trip all by itself. A few hundred metres of scrambling and easy climbing in a seriously impressive setting make this an absolutely brilliant quick hit. Views over to Forada, El Cid, the hinterland and Alicante can be enjoyed from the crest.

Access and parking

Exit the A-7 at El Campello and follow the CV-773 to Busot. Before arriving in Busot look out for signs for the Cueves de Canelobre, and follow these to the parking area immediately below the ridge. If this is full, drive back down the hill for a few hundred metres to a large lay-by and park there.

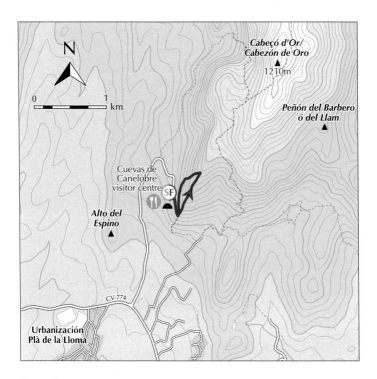

Approach

Walk past the café to the end of the road, where steps then lead up to the start of the via ferrata.

Note: Prior to setting off on the route, the abseil from the ridge comes down through the huge hole. The **yellow building** (toilet block) is a good point of reference because the hole can't be seen while on the ridge.

Cresta del Canelobre, Cabezón de Oro

II

III+

30m

20m

20m

Via ferrata section

Approach

Visitor centre and car park

Abseiling past the hole at the end of Cresta de la Cueva

The ridge

An easy and short via ferrata of 40m gains the ridge.

At the top of the via ferrata is a double-bolt belay on the ridge. Start the scramble proper from here.

1) III+, 45m This section is bolted, follow the ridge as it rises and narrows. Spike/block belays at various intervals.

2) III, 30m There is no fixed gear on this pitch, but a few slings will provide sufficient protection. Stay on the crest for maximum fun. Block belays.

3) II, 35m Move easily along the crest to a widening and block/thread belay.

4) II, 50m Easy scrambling up to a double-bolt abseil station on the south side (left) of the ridge, located immediately after a short rise.

Descent

The descent involves three abseils.

1) 30m Passes the mouth of a huge hole in the ridge to arrive on steep ledges. Go leftwards (looking out) to locate the next abseil station.

2) 20m Leads to a small stance.

3) 20m To the ground – beware of the spiky bushes on this one!

A vague path traverses left (facing outwards). Follow this as it takes a descending traverse line below crags, generally aiming for the café and parking area.

ROUTE 8

Forada Ridge

Start point	Parking area, Xorret de Cati, Elda/Petrer, ///modify.oval. supplemental
Grade	IV
Time	Total time 3hr 45min: approach 45min; route 2hr 30min; return 30min
Length	350m
Aspect/conditions	Sun all day
Equipment	50m rope, light trad rack with a few 120cm slings. Rock shoes optional
Abseils	The route involves two abseils of 25m and 17m

Tucked away in the Sierra del Maigmó, this stunning ridge has drawn climbers for many years. They have been coming to sample the well-bolted sport climbs that lie below either side of the ridge.

This is top-quality rock with occasional bolts but a trad feel and spectacular positions. Add to this the advantage of easy access. There are plenty of plus points – so get out there and do it!

Access and parking

Follow the A-31 motorway towards Madrid. At the twin towns of Elda/Petrer turn off at Elda junction just past a castle and signed for 'Centro Commercial'. Once off the motorway, turn right and right again at signs to the 'Xorret de Cati' hotel. Follow this road, as it clings to the side of a riverbed, for about 10km to a right turn, where you go right, and right again by large gateposts and a picnic area. Park here.

Approach

Continue on foot along this track, passing through almond groves and various terraces of cultivated land. Keep on this track until you reach an open area with a small ruin (about 15 minutes from the start). Go left at the 'Xorret de Cati'

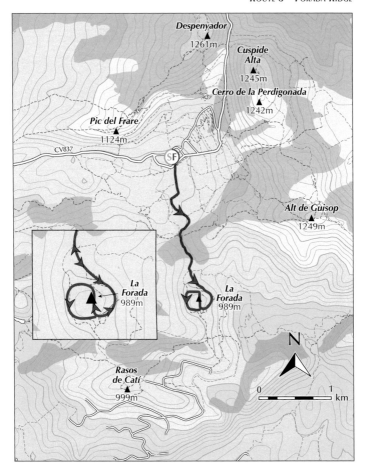

sign, then bear left at a rise and keep on this track to reach a minor col with an "Outdoor Activities" sign. From here take the wide track going rightwards, then, at a small outcrop on the right, take the left fork aiming for the left end of the ridge. Take the left branch (lower path) until the ridge comes down to meet the path. Turn right to follow the south side of the ridge, passing a small cave, to reach

61

Forada ridge – west side

IV

IV

Optional abseil
or down-climb →
at Grade IV

A 25m

A 17m

Return

Looking back to one of the towers on Forada

an open area in about
100m – and below easy
ground where the ridge
can be gained.

The ridge

Start with easy scram-
bling rightwards up to
gain a prominent notch.
From here follow the
ridge, easily at first, until
the rock steepens shortly
before a bolt. Climb the
fine arête at about grade
4 – passing a couple of
bolts before the terrain
levels again at a block
belay. A precarious
down-climb across to a
pinnacle is protected by
a couple of bolts. This
is easier than it looks,
but still requires care.

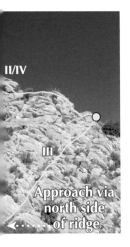

Approach via north side of ridge

Another option is to abseil 25m to reach the chain belay.

Move across blocks and slabs to gain steeper ground and ascend this to a widening in the ridge. Another long, narrow section leads to a single-bolt abseil.

Descend the south side of the ridge via a 17m abseil.

Descent
Walk under the south side of the crag as it descends, and follow paths leading around the 'toe' of the ridge to reach the north side and regain the outward route.

✪ ROUTE 9

Benicadell Ridge

Start point	Parking area, Casa de les Planisses, Beniatjar, ///rewinds. reflections.livened
Grade	IV+
Time	Total time 7hr 30min: approach 40min; ridge 6hr; descent 50min
Length	2km
Aspect/conditions	Initial pitch will have morning shade. Ridge has sun all day. Exposed to wind
Equipment	50m rope, helmet, harness, belay device, prussic cord, 5 quickdraws, alpine draws and a selection of slings. Some will find a light trad rack useful
Abseils	The route involves an 8m optional abseil

Beyond the steep crags of Bellus and rising from the fertile interior is this majestic rocky crest that lures intrepid adventurers. This is the most impressive ridge the region has to offer, being quite 'alpinesque' in scale. Even a fit and fast team will spend many hours on this one, with every minute savoured, for the scenery is outstanding and the exposure continually exhilarating.

Easy access and approach, along with interesting climbing and scrambling, make this a very worthwhile day out. Currently not overly popular with visiting climbers, but the tide will change so get in quick.

Access and parking

Follow the CV-60 inland from Gandía and turn onto the CV-615 at Castello de Rugat. Follow this through Rafol de Salem and on towards Beniatjar. Shortly before arriving at Beniatjar, and at a sharp bend in the road, turn left onto a dirt track marked with the sign 'Ombria del Benicadell'. Follow this as it winds uphill, keeping right at a junction, and continue to climb until you reach a parking area at Casa de les Planisses. About 15 minutes from the CV-615.

Approach

Continue on foot, through a vehicle barrier, and after 500m turn left to go steeply uphill on a concrete track. After 100m bear slight right onto a path by an old signpost. Follow the right-hand branch of this, passing a small pond, to gently descend parallel with the ridge for about 800m. There may be some fixed cable shortly before you arrive at the start of the climb.

The ridge

Start just left of a prominent orange recess, and traverse left, passing pegs to reach a bolt belay.

Ascend a groove to reach the ridge proper and continue along this for a few metres to a bolt belay.

The ridge continues for approximately 2km with much of it around grade III/ IV, mixed in with a few short sections of more difficult climbing up to about UK Severe. Stay on or as close to the crest as possible the whole time – this is narrow enough to make route-finding straightforward. The more difficult sections have some fixed protection but it's worthwhile having a small trad rack.

Shortly before arriving at the summit, you'll reach a short (8m) **abseil**. This bolted abseil was installed in 2019. It is possible and quite straightforward to scramble down the slab thus missing out the abseil.

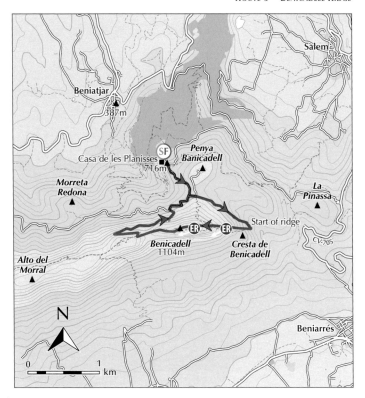

Immediately after the abseil is a prominent **gash of orange rock**. Climb just left of the gash and trend leftwards passing a bolt, before continuing straight up to pegs and a bolt. Big holds ease your passage through this steep terrain. This is the end of the difficulties, now continue along the widening crest to gain the summit **trig point**.

Escape options

There is an escape route down and left at about halfway. And then another at about three-quarters along, also on the left. Both are fairly obvious when encountered as they offer easy escape into the wide, vegetated gully. The gully can be followed to reach the summit, if desired.

Descent
From the summit, follow a good path (PR-CV 213.3) descending to a col, and turn right here, heading for the north side of the mountain. At a fingerpost, turn right, and descend to the wide track. Turn right onto this to reach Casa de les Planisses.

🚶 ROUTE 10
Arista al Forat de la Forada

Start point	Benissivá, ///blotched.bikes.orchestras
Grade	IV+
Time	Total time 4hr 40min: approach 40min; route 3hr; descent 1hr
Length	232m
Aspect/conditions	East-facing and relatively sheltered for a mountain route. Dries quickly. Approach walk is often in the shade, but the ridge gets sun until mid/late afternoon.
Equipment	50m single rope is plenty. A light trad rack with a selection of slings, medium-size cams and a few nuts
Abseils	The route involves a 15m abseil

Rising above the pretty Vall de Gallinera, this is part of a long, broad and rocky ridge. Few climbers venture into these mountains, but it has long been popular with walkers, many wanting to visit the huge *forat* (natural hole in the rock) at the summit. After a varied and adventurous climb the *forat* provides a fitting finale to the day.

There is a small amount of fixed gear, which helps route-finding, and most belays have a single bolt and thread (autumn 2019). The fixed gear on the pitches consists of threads, pegs and bolts, but are sparse, so take a light trad rack.

This is a large crag so expect to encounter loose rock, wear a helmet and be gentle with the rock. We are not aware of any other routes on the impressive north face…yet!

Originally climbed by father and son team, Javi Martin and Javi Martin Jnr on 2 September 2017, this is still a quiet place. The *forat* at the top is a popular spot with walkers.

Access and parking

From the N-332 take the CV-700 to Pego and continue inland on this road to reach the mountain village of Benissivá. Park considerately in the village.

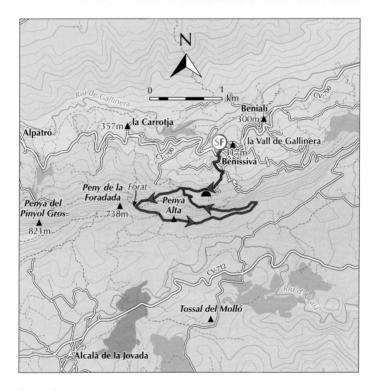

Approach

Mostly gentle uphill and all on good tracks/paths.

From the bakery in Benissivá, follow 'Forada' signs up through the village. Once clear of the village stay on the – mostly surfaced – lane, still following signs for 'Forada'. After about 25 minutes the lane becomes a path. Keep on this, aiming for the prominent hole in the mountain high above. After a couple of minutes, the path passes a cave on the left – it's worth a quick detour.

After about 35 minutes walking, and immediately after a right turn, turn right again at a 'Forada' sign onto a path running towards rocks and a large tree. Walk towards the tree then up a scree path and bear right to reach the base of the crag at the far side of a **pinnacle**.

The ridge

1) IV+, 27m Start below a corner with an in-situ thread a short way up. Climb to this and after about 10m trend slightly right towards an orange rock scar. Step left and directly up to a large ledge and bolt/thread belay.

2) IV, 25m Climb directly up from the belay, then trend slightly left to gain the ridge via a notch after about 12m. Then follow rocks left to a bolt/thread belay.

3) III, 20m Start just right of the belay and trend back left towards the crack after about 5m. Follow this to a large ledge and block belays.

4) (I) Walk rightwards to slabs and scramble up these diagonally right to regain the ridge left of a tree. Bolt belay.

5) IV+, 40m Climb the arête in a splendid position and continue directly and carefully up slabs to a bolt and thread belay when the ground eases.

6) III+, 40m Go left around a **pinnacle**, before climbing rightwards passing fixed gear. Continue trending right to easy ground and a block belay.

Easy scrambling leads rightwards, passing a col, to reach the final section.

7) III+, 40m Just left of a steep walk, scramble up to a groove and continue up this to regain the ridge. Follow this leftwards into another groove and over blocks to a large ledge and bolt belay.

The beckoning finale to Arista al Forat de la Forada

8) II, 40m Move right from the belay and follow scrambling terrain to a double-bolt belay above the **forat**.

A **15m abseil** reaches the ground.

Descent

From the summit, follow the main PR hiking route heading towards the coast. After a few minutes turn left to follow a good path descending the north side of the mountain. This re-joins the approach route and offers splendid views of the ridge.

 # ROUTE 11

Cresta dels Bardals, Serrella

Start point	Water deposit beyond Casa Polselli, Port de Confrides, Confrides, ///growing.redeem.oval
Grade	IV+
Time	Total time 3hr 40min: approach 25min; route 3hr; return 15min
Length	300m
Aspect/conditions	Sunny all day but due to altitude can be windy
Equipment	50m rope, light trad rack with plenty of 120cm slings, medium cams
Abseils	The route involves a 10m abseil

Perched high up in the Serrella mountains, next to the stunning summit of Pla de la Casa, this ridge offers big views. Being so high up, you might expect a long approach walk. In fact, it's only 25 minutes. The ridge itself can be tackled in a short day and offers exciting and exposed scrambling along a very narrow crest. There is loose rock, so we recommend this ridge only to more experienced parties. Also, most of the route is a traverse, so all members need to be of equal ability and comfortable on very exposed terrain. While a grade of IV+ has been given, this helps represent the exposed and serious nature of the terrain rather than the difficulty of the climbing.

Access and parking

From the coast follow the CV-70 through Guadalest and continue on this road as it winds its way up into the mountains. Turn off the CV-70 between the 18km and 19km marking at Port de Confrides, and go immediately past Casa Polselli on a concrete road. Follow this good, but mostly unsurfaced road for about 3km to reach a large green container (water deposit). It is possible to park here, or…continue along the wide track as it descends towards the rocky summit of 'Pla de la Casa'. The ridge will soon be visible on the right. Park at a crossroads marked by a walkers' sign for Castell de Castells and Confrides.

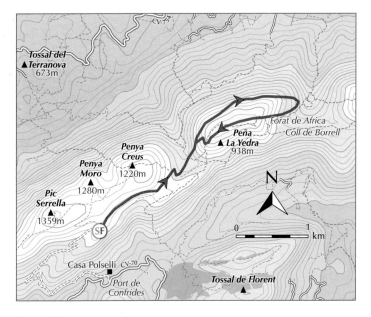

Approach

Continue on foot along the wide track going downhill, passing a ruin on the left. After a few minutes turn sharp right, still descending, then soon go left to follow under the ridge, with the 'Pla de la Casa' summit ahead. At **Coll de Borrell** join a path on the right to ascend rocky scrub up to the start.

Cresta dels Bardals

Descent

Parking

Route around
back of ridge

Prominent
notch

10m

Coll de
Borrell

Approach

Knife edge is what Cresta dels Bardals is all about

Forat de Africa/Recingle Finestra is just left of the start of the ridge and well worth the short diversion to have a look before setting off.

The ridge
From where the ridge aims down towards the Coll de Borrell, walk around the initial section on its right-hand side, and gain the ridge proper as soon as it's possible.

1) IV+, 45m Almost immediately the ridge becomes a sharp crest. There are two bolts along this section, before it rises to reach another bolt. Belay here.

2) IV, 30m Climb easily up to regain the crest and continue traversing. When you get to a large pinnacle, descend by squeezing past this to reach a vegetated col.
Walk/scramble across the col to reach the next rocks.

3) III, 15m Belay on large blocks, then move up onto the ridge, and follow the crest to a three-bolt belay/abseil.

4) 10m Abseil into the **prominent notch**. There is one bolt at the notch, but threads are easily found to back this up.

5) III, 10m Climb directly up to regain the crest in increasingly exposed positions. Easy climbing leads to a two-bolt belay. The way ahead is enticing.

6) III, 30m Follow the crest in a sensational position for 30m to reach a thread/boulder belay.

7) III, 40m Follow the crest until it widens slightly. Belay on blocks.

8) II, 40m The ridge begins to descend gently towards a large plateau. Belay on blocks on the plateau.

Descent
Walk along the plateau, keeping the ridge on your left. Follow vague paths through pine woodland to reach the parking area at the signpost.

ROUTE 12
Cresta del Castellar

Start point	Roadside parking, Calle de la Serreta, Alcoy, ///casually. starred.dogs
Grade	4+ (the route is fully bolted, hence the sport-climbing grade)
Time	Total time 2hr 35min: approach 5min; route 2hr 15min; return 15min
Length	115m climbing, 200m scrambling
Aspect/conditions	Sun from late morning. Sheltered
Equipment	50m rope, 12 quickdraws

With straightforward access from the Alicante area and a very short approach walk, as well as being easy to combine with a walk through the Barranco del Cint to see the vultures, there is plenty to recommend this fine ridge. Almost roadside, very well bolted, top-quality rock and fine positions all add to make this a perfect mini-adventure. The setting is on the edge of a large town, giving an urban feel. Still, it is a quiet venue, and venturing into Barranco del Cint afterwards can give more of a wilderness feel.

Access and parking
Take the A-7 motorway and turn off at Alcoy. Follow the N-340 leading through this large town to the CV-795. Turn right onto Calle de la Serreta in the suburb of Batoy and follow this as it skirts around the edge of an industrial estate, then go left to reach roadside parking immediately below the prominent ridge.

Approach
From the road, locate a track – this may have a chain across it – and follow this as it leads through pine and olive trees towards the base of the ridge. Cresta del Castellar is the large, left-hand ridge.

Cresta del Castellar

Descent walk

II 200m

4+

4

4

Approach path

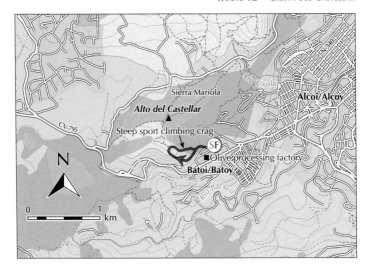

The ridge

1) 4, 35m Start a few metres right of the base of the ridge and follow bolts as they trend left then right to join the ridge proper. Double-bolt belay on a spacious stance.

2) 4, 40m Move left then right to regain the ridgeline and follow the crest in an increasingly exposed position to reach another double-bolt belay below a steep wall.

3) 4+, 40m Steep moves off the belay lead to easy ground and another finely positioned stance offering a mix of urban and mountain views – maybe unique in the region. A few metres further back is another double-bolt belay, worth a quick pitch to here before coiling the ropes. The large ledge to the left (looking up) is a great vantage point.

4) II, 200m Ascend directly to the ridge and follow it for about 200m where the ridge merges with the hillside.

Descent

From the top of the ridge follow a path descending rightwards, but then soon weaves back under the ridge and back to the road.

ROUTE 13

Cresta del Maigmó

Start point	Lay-by beside CV-805, near Agost, ///shop.squares. overpayment
Grade	IV
Time	Total time 3hr: approach 15 mins; route 2 hr; return 45 min
Length	700m
Aspect/conditions	Sun all day. Exposed to the wind
Equipment	30m rope (minimum), helmet, harness, belay device, prussic cord. A selection of slings, medium cams and nuts may be found useful, although for the confident/ competent these may not be necessary

This is a fine introductory ridge scramble, offering very rapid access and incredible views. The rock is typical of ridges in the area, with some loose rock mixed in with the solid. With care you will find an abundance of great rock. There is virtually no fixed gear on this outing – unusual for any rocky ground in Costa Blanca; there's only one old peg on the whole route. So this can definitely be considered a proper trad day – and a good place to practice skills. Exposure is considerable from fairly early on and builds pleasantly.

Access and parking

Take the A-7 motorway from Alicante towards Alcoy and turn off onto the CV-827 signed for Urbanización de Maigmó. Follow this for a few hundred metres until a left turning for Agost leads back under the motorway. Take this and shortly after go straight across at a roundabout and almost immediately turn sharp right onto the CV-805. This soon runs parallel to the motorway. After about 350m and immediately before the prominent left bend in the road, park at a small lay-by on the right.

Approach

Vague paths lead from the lay-by up towards a large green water tank and into pine woodland. From above the **water tank**, pick any of many small paths leading

Cresta del Maigmó

Finishing col

Descent

II

Section 2

Prominent pine tree

Section 1

IV (max)

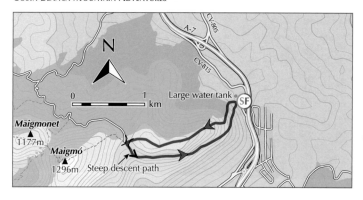

towards the base of the ridge, reached in about 10 minutes, only 300m from the road.

The ridge

Broad and easy angled rocks mark the initially vague rock ridge. This soon narrows and begins to feel like the proper ridge it is. Pick a line and go for it – keeping left gives maximum value.

After around 400m of scrambling, with short sections of easy climbing, a **prominent pine** is reached at an easing. Walk up a gentle scree slope to gain the next section of ridge. Start this on the left side and regain the crest.

Another 300m of easier scrambling remains as the ridge begins to broaden once more and merges with the mountain at a wide **col**. This marks the end of the ridge and is a finely positioned spot to enjoy the view.

Escape options

A multitude of escape options on either side.

Descent

From the col go left down a steep, vague path. This may look improbable at first, but it does improve, a little. Within about 50m of setting off, you will reach a short section with fixed rope. Use this to negotiate a rock step then trend left (looking out) continuing to follow faint animal paths.

A descending traverse leftwards under the ridge gains the third, steep, scree-filled gully. Zigzag down this to reach open scree and scrub. Keep going left and descend as much as possible to reach better ground and the roadside.

Allow at least one hour for the descent.

VIA FERRATAS

Crossing one of the many bridges on the Callosa de Segura via ferrata (Route 18)

VIA FERRATAS

In recent years via ferratas have really taken off in this region. In fact, it is difficult to keep up with development and, at time of writing, a number of proposals are in the pipeline for more.

A via ferrata is a quick way to cover very steep mountain terrain, typically vertical rock faces. A cable will be in place to clip into and large metal staples aid passage. A few routes included here involve abseils as part of the descent. There is no long history here as there is in the Italian Dolomites, and all routes have been installed with mountain fun in mind. So the routes and fixed equipment are mostly in excellent condition. Local authorities are often involved with funding and upkeep.

Equipment recommendations

Harness, helmet, via ferrata lanyard, gloves, water, food. We also recommend carrying a rope and belay device on any via ferrata, in case of emergency. Via ferrata lanyards are available to purchase in the numerous Decathlon stores (for example Ondara, Gandia, Benidorm, Alicante), www.decathlon.es, or try www.egruta.com, an independent and generally well-stocked climbing shop in the town of La Nucia with very helpful owners.

Grading

Routes in this section have been graded according to the Hüsler system. For comparisons with other grading systems, see theuiaa.org/mountaineering/via-ferrata.

- **K1:** Easy access, very well equipped and little exposure.
- **K2:** Easy access, requiring more athletic manoeuvres and good balance.
- **K3:** Steeper terrain and equipment often more spaced. Good physical fitness required.
- **K4:** Often in mountainous terrain with very steep sections, but typically well equipped. Navigation and other mountaineering skills may be required. High level of physical fitness required.
- **K5:** As K4 but covering more technical/steeper terrain.

Ⓑ ROUTE 14
Penya del Figueret

Start/finish	Lay-bys at Penya del Figueret, Relleu, ///accumulated. lefthander.mazelike
Grade	K2
Time	Total time 2hr 30min: approach 20min; route 1hr 30min; return 40min
Length	300m
Aspect/conditions	Sun all day. Descent offers shade
Equipment	60m rope for the abseil
Abseils	The route involves a 30m abseil
Note	The via ferrata is closed annually between 1 Dec and 31 May due to nesting birds. See the information board at the start for further details and any changes.

Installed during 2016, this is one of the newer additions to the region. It is very well equipped and proves to be an excellent, easily accessible via ferrata, with good variety and an airy ridge traverse to finish.

Access and parking

From Finestrat, follow the CV-758 towards Sella, then turn onto the CV-775 towards Relleu. Upon entering Relleu keep to the left, following the by-pass, then re-join the CV-775 on the south side of the village. Take the second right – signed Figueret – and follow this surfaced lane to reach a small parking place next to a modern bungalow and right-hand road junction.

Approach
Continue on foot taking the right-hand lane, which soon leads to an information board. Just beyond is a small path heading uphill on the left. Follow this cairned path to the base of the crag near its right-hand end.

The via ferrata
The cable begins well before the route leaves the ground. This is helpful for anyone new to the activity as it allows time to get accustomed to using lanyards. The

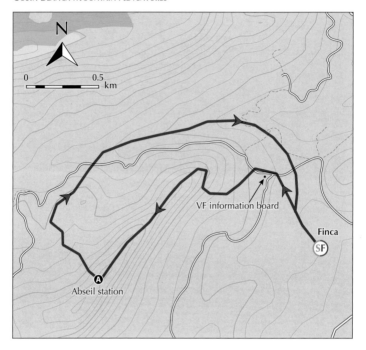

staples are spaced close together, so it is never necessary to use the rock. The cable is always nearby, and is fixed to the wall at regular intervals, so giving an increased element and feeling of safety.

Chains have been fitted on the traverse sections, where they act as handrails and feel reassuring. Towards the top the gradient eases and you reach the ridge. This is a fine vantage point to admire the Puig Campana. The cable continues along the ridge before trending right to reach a double-bolt abseil station. There is another abseil station about 10m further on. A **30m abseil** follows.

Descent

A 30m abseil descends the loose slope. It's well worth keeping a helmet on here!

Follow the small path downhill and soon cables appear again. This is now a path, but it's slippery, so worth clipping in. At the edge of the woods the cable ends. You then continue on the small path downhill and into the woods to reach the road. Turn right onto the road to return to the parking area.

Penya del Figueret

30m abseil to descent path

Descent path

Approach

ROUTE 15
Ponoch (Ponoig)

Start/finish	Parking area at the end of Calle Camino del Flare, La Nucia, ///regiment.count.tousles
Grade	K4; scramble grade 2–3 (optional)
Time	Total time 3hr 30min: approach 30min; route 2hr 30min; return 30min. Add 2 hours on to the total time if including the scramble.
Length	250m via ferrata, 300m scramble (optional)
Aspect/conditions	All-day sun. Final section of scramble and initial part of descent go into the shade from early afternoon
Equipment	60m rope is required for the abseils
Abseils	The route involves two 20m abseils or one 40m abseil if using the upper abseils after the scramble. There is also one 25m and one 30m abseil for the final two abseils that form part of the descent from the VF. The 30m abseil is only just doable on a 60m rope

A relatively new installation with recently renewed (2019) cables to boot. The crag of Ponoch is enormous and this via ferrata seeks a way up the impressive face on its right-hand side. There are a number of sustained steep sections and exposure builds rapidly. At the top, some scrambling and a double abseil descent complete the journey. There is an optional continuation to the summit plateau.

Access and parking

From the N-332 follow signs for La Nucia. Follow the CV-70 around the out-skirts of La Nucia and turn left at the third roundabout on the town by-pass. This leads into a new *urbanización* on Avenida Balcón de Ponoig. Follow this road through the housing estate, turning left at the top (next to a shallow water channel) to reach a large car park by a large green building.

There is a via ferrata information board here, and it also provides approach details and general information.

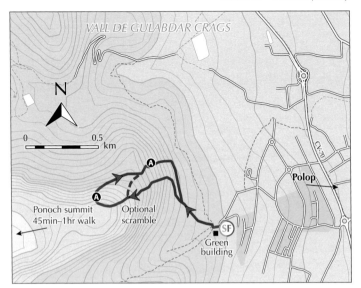

Approach
Follow a path over the water channel and into the pine woodland. Yellow, red and sometimes green dots mark the way on a small path leading to an arête towards the right-hand end of the crag.

The via ferrata
The way ahead is clear. The rungs are mostly quite close together, but be prepared for the occasional 'reachy' section. There are a couple of traverses which add to the sense of exposure. After most of the steep sections, convenient ledges appear. It's always worth taking a breather on these before ploughing onwards on the skyward quest. When the angle eventually eases and you reach the top, huge swathes of rock still loom above, but the cable terminates here. It is now time to find the way down unless you're wanting to complete the continuation scramble to the summit.

Descent
Follow a rough path uphill towards a large boulder. Just before reaching this, turn right, and aim for a solitary tree. Soon the path heads downhill and becomes rockier. There are a few sections equipped with cable, so keep the lanyards on. A

Ponoch via ferrata and scramble

Top of via ferrata

To the abseils

Descent

Via ferrata

Approach

To the abseils

Continuation scramble to summit plateau

Enjoying exposed scrambling high on Ponoch with Echo valley, Sanchet, and the Serrella mountains as a backdrop

hard-to-spot signpost points out the top, very well-equipped abseil station, from where you will make the first of two abseils.

1) 25m Leads to a large ledge, able to fit half a dozen in comfort.

2) 30m To the ground. This one has a slightly overhanging section near the bottom.

Important safety note: The information board and a small in-situ sign both suggest the second abseil is 35m! We have only ever used a 60m rope for these abseils, so suggest the lengths to be first: 25m; second: 30m. And remember to tie a knot in the end of your rope!

Optional scramble

From the top of the via ferrata follow the path for a few metres before trending left, but keeping right of some slabs, and continue up to the castellated ridge. For maximum exposure stay on the crest and follow this rightwards in outstanding positions. Aim for a cluster of trees that occupy a slight depression, pass to the right side of these and continue ascending to another cluster of trees via a pleasant corner/groove. Trend left above here.

The continuation is now marked by a fixed rope (2019). Follow this leftwards through occasionally tricky terrain. Due to the sharp nature of the rock hereabouts, it is worth checking the condition of any fixed ropes before using them. After about 25m the rope ends and the difficulties are behind you. Traverse left with ease to reach rockier ground once more. Ascend this, trending left at the cairn below a rib, and quickly up to easy ground on the edge of a plateau.

To reach the summit of Ponoch

Pick a route through the jumble of rocks and small buttresses, mostly easy, but also loose! After about 10 minutes of steady uphill progress you'll reach the plateau. This is pathless, rough and rocky. The easiest way is to keep on the higher

Ponoch - scramble detail

Walk to summit of mountain 45min - 1hr ·····▶

To via ferrata abseils ·····▶

Walk to abseils ·····▶

Bolts and maybe an in-situ rope

From top of via ferrata ·····

and rockier ground. Animal tracks cross the plateau, these are only worth following for short distances and when they are going toward the summit, otherwise it's best to give them a miss. Keep on an upward trajectory until you reach the summit.

Although the plateau gives some rough walking, the views more than make up for it. To the right are the magnificent cliffs of Xanchet and Vall de Gulabdar, with Aitana and Serrella beyond and dominating the distant skyline. Look left for close-up views of Puig Campana. And once on the summit, the castellated ridge of El Realet will catch your attention. From here look back across the huge plateau to marvel at the Bernia ridge, and down to all those now small-looking towns and villages dotting the coastline.

Descent from the summit
From the summit follow the well-marked PR-CV 13.1 as it descends to the Coll de Llamp. Turn left (south) at the Coll de Llamp to descend onto the PR-CV 17. At the next signpost turn left again following the Polop (per Cigarri) route that traverses back below the summit of Ponoch. This pleasant and well-marked track soon arrives at Coll del Cigarri. Continue the descent into a broad valley with increasing pine woodlands. The huge cliffs to the left are what you were walking above when up on the plateau! This track leads all the way back to the parking area.

Descent from the top of the scramble (omitting the summit)
If you don't want to visit the summit or if you're short on time, there is a quicker, albeit more technical descent from the top of the scramble.

After the steeper, scrambling terrain gives way to more walkable mountain terrain and the edge of the plateau, walk uphill trending slightly right to locate cairns marking the entrance to a large bay with a concave wall of orange/yellow rock on the far side. Scramble down into the bay and follow a vague path leading over to a grey wall and a clump of trees. There is an equipped abseil station (double-bolt) next to the trees. Either a single abseil of 40m or two 20m abseils will reach the scree slope below. The intermediate abseil station is also well equipped with double-bolt belay.

From here descend scree slopes to join the descent as for the via ferrata.

ROUTE 16
El Cid

Start/finish	Road head at Casica del Forestal, Elda/Petrer, ///tennis. rebukes.fluidly
Grade	K4
Time	Total time 3hr 40min: approach 40min; route 2hr; return 1hr
Length	Approximately 300m of vertical height gain
Aspect/conditions	North-facing, can be chilly
Equipment	Standard VF kit

This is a long and exciting via ferrata with sections requiring rock-climbing skills. While steep and challenging at times, it does relent, with short sections of walking/scrambling. The final section in particular offers tremendous atmosphere and exposure. It finishes within a few metres of the huge summit cairn of El Cid (1152m).

Access and parking

Take the A-31 motorway from Alicante towards Madrid. After about 15 minutes take the Petrer/Salinas exit that leads onto a minor road running alongside the motorway. Stay on this road as it veers right, heading uphill towards the large rock face ahead (south face of El Cid) until you reach a parking area (not well signed) at Casica del Forestal, at the end of the road.

Approach

From the car park follow the wide track going uphill northeast. After about 30 minutes this track begins to descend at a sharp turning, look out for 2 small cairns on the right and a cable above. This is the start of the via ferrata. Note that this is on the north face of the mountain.

The via ferrata

At about 300m of vertical ascent this is one of the longer via ferratas in the region. All the difficult sections are well protected with cable. There are staples for some

El Cid via ferrata

Descent from summit on well-marked path

Approach from parking

K4

ER

K3

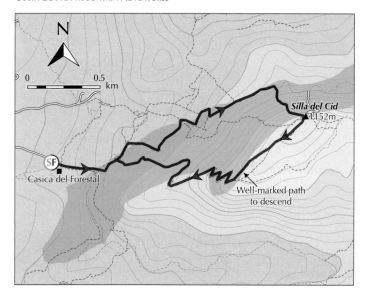

but not all of the route, so time will be spent on the rock, definitely adding to the fun and the challenge.

The ascent is broken into sections and at about half-height there is an escape route to the right.

At a junction of cables, follow the more direct line upwards rather than the easy traverse across left. (This is a section under construction 2020.)

The route finishes on the summit of El Cid – 1152m, and a wonderful vantage point.

Descent
Follow the well-marked PR route descending towards Petrer, the large town visible far below.

ROUTE 17
Redován

Start/finish	Public swimming pool parking area, Calle del Seminarista Ballesta, Redován, ///antiquated. undoubtedly.acorns
Grade	K2 (initial section); K5 (upper section)
Time	Total time 3hr 15min: approach 15min; route 2hr; return 1hr. If only attempting the lower section, total time will be nearer 1hr and 30min.
Length	700m total for both sections
Aspect/conditions	Sun all day. No shelter, can be very hot
Equipment	Standard VF kit

Newly installed in 2018, the Redován via ferrata climbs 'La Pancha' (the belly) and considerably upped the game for via ferratas in the region. It is a fine, impressive and continually interesting route, with planning and thought for most age groups and abilities. Easy access from the A-7 motorway and Alicante Airport, makes for an even more tempting activity on an airport day.

Access and parking
Parking is on Calle del Seminarista Ballesta next to the sports centre and public swimming pool on the northeast side of Redován and almost directly below the huge cliff. From the Calpe/Alicante direction follow the A-7 south, turning off at the junction with the N-340, and from here follow signs for Redován.

Approach
From the parking area follow a good track uphill and towards the cliff. Soon there are signposts showing the way to the via ferrata.

Initial section
After an easy introduction up a well-equipped wall, there comes a straightforward traverse over steep ground, that leads to the first of four bridges. Each bridge has its own character and challenge. Linking the bridges are further stapled sections,

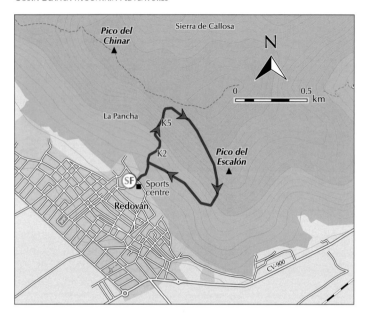

some being steep, but not sustained. This whole section (K2) has relatively low exposure levels and is suitable for adventurous youngsters. An inscription on a large rock indicates the top of this initial section. From here you can choose to continue to the upper cliff or descend back to the valley.

Descent
From the top of the initial via ferrata there is a small path going rightwards back down the hill. It is about 15 minutes' walk to the parking area.

Second section
For those continuing to the top, turn left at the top of the first section, follow a small path leading under the main cliff. Soon you will find the next equipped section. This is immediately steep (K5) and remains so for much of the way. A long diagonal ramp leading rightwards provides the first respite for tired arms. Soon after you'll reach a resting station. Take a moment here to soak up the view and situation. Now another very steep section (K5) leads to what looks like a **giant hinge**. There are two ways to progress through this section.
1   Follow the staples leftwards, thus bypassing the 'hinge'.

Redován via ferrata

Descent path

45m bridge

Ladder

Hinge

K5

Initial section K2

Descent from K2 section

The hinge swing

2   Using the chains, pull the hinge to you and clip into the snapgate carabiner (make sure to keep your lanyards attached to the independent cable at all times) and swing across the void. Both choices are fun, but the hinge swing is the way to go!

More upper body exercise leads up to an **enclosed section of ladder**. Here the staples end, briefly, so turn to face the valley far below and climb the ladder, at its top is another resting station. Be thankful for it!

Easier sections lie ahead, with a fantastically airy traverse rightwards that terminates at a 45m bridge linking with the other side of the mountain. This is a grand finale, best enjoyed on a calm day. Once over the bridge the equipped section continues for a short way and leads directly to the descent route.

Descent

From the top a signpost points to the right. Follow this and the green and white paint to stay on the good and occasionally exposed path as it weaves its way towards a col and back to the parking area. Note, there are also green and white markings leading uphill from the top of the via ferrata to the top of the mountain.

ROUTE 18
Callosa de Segura

Start/finish	Cueva Ahumada recreation area, Callosa de Segura, /// defraud.airsick.roundabout
Grade	First section K3; second section K5
Time	Total time 3hr 30min: approach 15min; both sections of via ferrata 3hr; descent 15min (first section only total time 1hr 30min)
Length	1150m
Aspect/conditions	Sun all day, no shade or shelter. Can be very hot
Equipment	Standard VF kit

Opened in February 2020 this is the newest via ferrata in the region and the second longest on the Iberian Peninsula. It is also the most challenging. So, if planning to complete the whole round, it is well worth taking refreshments. For those not wanting to do the more challenging section, the initial section is more friendly and still good fun, with around three bridge-crossings and plenty of staples to climb. This initial section would make a good first via ferrata trip and is suitable for adventurous children with their parents. The tough section (referred to as *tramo deportivo*) is not suitable for youngsters or anyone without a good head for heights. It is long, strenuous and demanding, with considerable sections of steep down-climbing.

Access and parking

Heading south from Alicante on the A-7 motorway, take the exit for Callosa/Granja/Cox onto the CV-900. Follow this through the small town of Callosa de Segura. Before reaching Redován – the next town – the road passes under a railway bridge. Turn right immediately after this into the recreation area. Follow the dirt track for about 100m to reach a large parking area and the via ferrata information board.

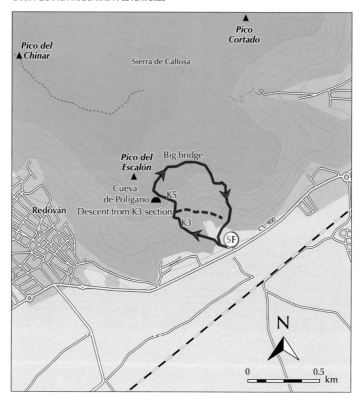

Approach

Follow the riverbed upstream until a path crosses the riverbed. Head uphill and past some huge boulders. Go left here following red painted posts to reach the start.

Initial section

After a short section of easy climbing you will reach the first bridge. Cross this to an easier section with fixed chain.

Another bridge reaches a 'postman's walk' (wire bridge) before a traverse leads to another bridge. This is quickly followed by another 'postman's walk'.

Callosa de Segura via ferrata

Overhanging down-climb

Descent

96m bridge

Descent after initial section

K5

Cueva de Polígano

K3

Approach

Looking up to the high bridge – spot the figure!

A short down-climb leads to end of the K3 section with markers showing the return route, should this be required.

Second section

Those here for a more serious challenge will be carrying on. It all gets a bit wild now. The route climbs the left side of the massive **Cueva de Polígono** (cave) all the way to the summit. This is about 100m and mostly vertical.

At the top a short bridge forms the continuation, although if busy this is easily by-passed with a walk-around option. Over to the right is the next challenge, and one best saved for a calm day. At 96m this **bridge** feels and is long – as it spans the void to the other side of the mountain. Be prepared for some wobble!

Another small bridge reaches a small cave, then an easy descent leads to the first section of strenuous, overhanging, down-climbing. Remember to use feet wisely on these sections.

A long traverse section is equipped with chains, and this too is strenuous. Another 'postman's walk' bridge and down-climb lead to the final traverse. Take a breather here – it isn't quite in the bag yet.

The final **overhanging down-climb** is seriously steep and traverses slightly as it goes. The ground is close, you can do it!

Descent

A good track leads back to the recreation area.

ROUTE 19
Castillo Salvatierra

Start/finish	Las Cruces recreation area, Villena, ///foam.dribble. moved
Grade	K2
Time	Total time 2hr: approach 15min; route 1hr 30min; return 15min
Length	400m
Aspect/conditions	Predominantly faces southwest and is high enough to catch the sun for much of the day. It finishes on a minor summit which may offer a cooling breeze. Even though this is high up, the two main roads far below do generate some traffic noise.
Equipment	Standard VF kit

Being one of the easiest via ferratas in the region and updated during autumn 2020, this is a good place to start for anyone new to the activity. Particular attention has been paid to the initial section that feels tailor-made for newcomers. Recent development has seen this installation extended considerably, making it now a much more worthwhile trip for anyone staying in the Alicante area. There are no abseils so a rope and technical climbing skills are not obligatory.

Easy access, with fairly low levels of exposure and with continuous interest, together mean this via ferrata attracts plenty of visitors, including organised activity groups.

Access and parking

Follow the A-31 motorway (toll free) towards Madrid. Turn off at Villena and follow signs for Centro Histórico. Go left at the traffic lights, then right at a roundabout towards Castell Atalaya. Soon bear right and right again to Las Cruces recreation area where there is a large parking area above the castle and town. This is a fine vantage point.

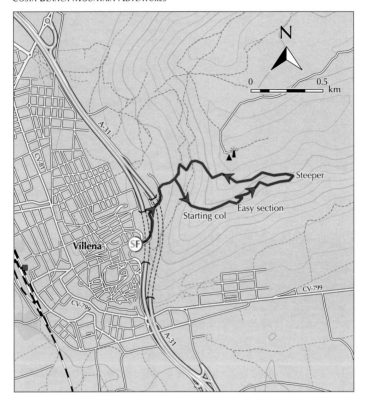

Approach

Opposite the parking area is a signpost showing various walking routes. Follow 'Route 19' for the via ferrata. This zigzags up the hillside for about five minutes, following yellow/white paint markings, and generally trends leftwards away from the parking area. At the next signpost turn right, keeping to the via ferrata sign. This leads steeply up to a rocky col, be prepared for some easy scrambling here. Once at the col, green paint marks the start on the left.

The via ferrata

Traverse and descend easy ground. This passes an equipped steep section; ignore this and continue to the next steep ladder section. After that slow start, this is

Castillo Salvatierra via ferrata

Descent

Steeper from here

K2

Approach over col

Equipped from here; very easy

High wire crossing

where the route gets spicy. Climb the ladder and negotiate a variety of traverses, more steep sections and two wire bridges in spectacular positions. All the while the route is leading back leftwards to top out near **red and white aerials**. Along the way are numerous rest places, so it is easy to stop and admire the view. The end of the equipped section comes all too quickly, but it does finish on a summit with incredible views. Late afternoon is a particularly good time of day to be finishing as sunset up there is especially beautiful.

Descent
Shortly before the aerials, look out for large blobs of green paint. Follow these back to the starting col. Initially the terrain is rocky and quite scrambly, but soon eases as the col nears.

ROUTE 20

Aventador

Start/finish	Woodland parking near Alboi, Genovés, ///exits.biscuit. technical
Grade	K3
Time	Total time 1hr: approach 10min; route 25min; return 25min
Length	60m
Aspect/conditions	West/shady until mid-afternoon. Perfect for cool winter days, but equally suitable on a warm spring morning before the sun cooks it.
Equipment	Standard VF kit

The climbing sections are often busy at weekends and during holidays, but the via ferrata is usually quiet.

Access and parking

From the south, follow the N-332 through the bustling town of Oliva. At the northern end of town turn left towards Font d'en Carros. Follow the twisting road through this town then turn right onto the CV-683 to Beniflá. Go left at the roundabout and straight ahead at the next to reach the CV-60 heading for Xátiva. This is a good dual carriageway. Stay on this until the CV-610 and turn right here towards Lluxent. Keep with the CV-610 as it passes through Quatretonda then to Genovés. Go through Genovés and, at the second roundabout on the south side of town, turn left and, after only a few metres, take the first turning on the right at a sign for Alboi. Follow this for about 2km, and then immediately after crossing the railway, turn sharp left. At a T-junction turn left and follow this lane for about 1.5km to a large parking area in woodland.

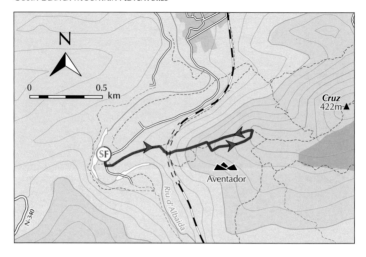

Approach

From the parking area continue along the unsurfaced track leading uphill, and after a couple of hundred metres, when the crag is already in view, take a path on the right, and follow this as it rises gently towards the crag. Ignore any paths leading off leftwards, and keep to the main path up to the base of the crag. The via ferrata is located at the extreme left end of the crag, after it changes aspect (from south to west facing).

The via ferrata

Steep and unrelenting, the route takes in the full height of the crag on well-spaced staples. Its persistent steepness means good technique will be rewarded. The equipped section terminates on a ridge with splendid views over the river and valley. Scramble along the left side of the ridge for a short way to begin the descent.

Descent

A vague path traverses through vegetation, descending slightly as it goes. This soon turns left to descend more steeply towards a scree path leading back under the crag and to the base.

Sports climbs on the crag

This crag also offers some fine sport climbs. A topo and brief description is included here for those wanting to sample the climbing.

3 **BA** 5, 28m Climb the flake, making tricky moves left to below the bushes. Climb between the bushes before trending slightly right to the top.

4 **Asterix** 5+, 28m From the tip of a flake, climb past the pale rock then skirt past the overhang on its left to reach the top.

5 **Idefix** 5+, 26m Climb slabs left of the orange rock and past the right edge of an overhang to gain the top.

6 **Rafa** 5, 26m Climb just left of the bubbly crack line. Aim just right of the orange rock and continue to gain a groove leading to a lower-off.

7 **Pepe** 5, 26m Climb a vague rib, trending left then right to reach a lower-off shared with Dit.

8 **Dit** 5, 26m Climb bubbly rock to the bush, keep left of this, then go right into the prominent groove. Climb this with interest, and go left up slabs to finish.

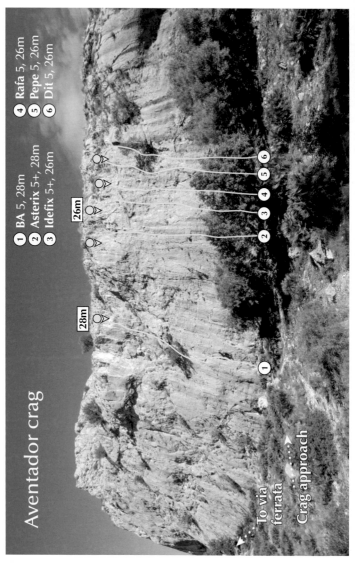

Aventador crag

1 BA 5, 28m
2 Asterix 5+, 28m
3 Idefix 5+, 26m

4 Rafa 5, 26m
5 Pepe 5, 26m
6 Dit 5, 26m

28m

26m

To via ferrata

Crag approach

CANYONS

The final abseil in Barranco
del Infierno (Route 22)

🌐 CANYONS

The following canyons are tucked away out of sight and they all lead to peaceful, adventurous places deep in the mountains. It is rare to have company in even the most popular canyon – the Infierno. And while this isn't canyoning in the traditional sense, where getting wet and swimming are obligatory, these dry *barrancos* offer their own charm and attraction.

Documented here are a selection of the finest. Some are short trips that can be squeezed into a morning or afternoon, while others will be full days and involve multiple abseils of up to 50m.

All the canyons can be enjoyed wet or dry, we describe all here assuming dry conditions. If there has been recent heavy rain, wetsuits, dry bags, lots of swimming, and a different skill set will be needed.

To find out about other canyons in the region, go to www.celaontiny-ent.es (Spanish only, but the best reliable source of information).

Season

The optimum time to visit is October–April inclusive. Avoid all the canyons described during or after heavy or prolonged rainfall and do not proceed if there is flowing water.

Grading

The routes in this section have been graded using the French canyon grading system for verticality. As all canyon trips in the guide are described for when conditions are dry, the aquatic (A) grading is not applicable.

- **V1:** Very easy. No abseils or down-climbing.
- **V2:** Easy. Abseils are less than 10m and anchors are easily reached. Any down-climbs are straightforward.
- **V3:** A little difficult. Abseils are typically less than 30m and down-climbs will be no more than 3+ (French sport grade).
- **V4:** Quite difficult. Involves longer abseils of 30m+ with some anchors being difficult to reach/ropes difficult to set up. Climbing sections may require aid techniques at grade A0 and/or 4 (an A0 grade may require the climber to pull on a fixed piece of gear or step up in a sling etc)
- **V5:** Difficult. Multiple long abseils of 30m+ and hanging belays will be encountered.

ROUTE 21

Barranco del Pas de Tancat

Start/finish	CV-715 Bolulla to Tarbena road, Bolulla, ///degradation. incubator.span
Grade	V4
Time	Total time 4hr 20min: approach 50min; route 3hr; return 30min
Length	1km
Equipment	Harness, helmet, abseil device and prussic, 60m rope (minimum), 1 x 120cm sling

An easily accessible canyon in the savagely cut gorge below Castell de Garx. Using one vehicle, as we have described here, is straightforward; but if you want less walking time, you can take two vehicles and leave one at Col de Garx.

A wilderness experience is guaranteed on this trip, with minimal likelihood of seeing or hearing anything other than local wildlife.

Access and parking

Take the CV-715 Tarbena to Bolulla road, between Km45 and Km46 look out for a sharp turning to the right (when coming downhill) on a hairpin bend. Turn right off the main road here and follow the narrow, surfaced lane for about 2km. Park considerately by a green bridge.

Approach

Continue on foot along the lane up to the **Col de Garx** (about 30 minutes). From the Col, descend the wide track for a few minutes until you reach a sharp turning on the right. Take this turning and walk through the olive groves. Go past the sharp left turn and soon the track bears right again and crosses a gentle valley. Follow the lower path – marked with a red dot on a tree. Soon it becomes vague and overgrown, but a further red dot marks the start of the final descent, moving right along a narrow channel.

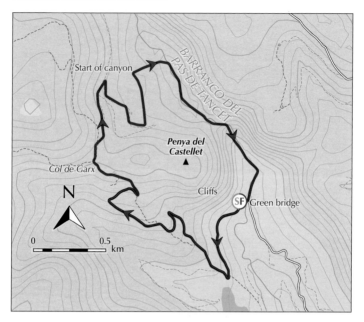

The canyon

Barranco del Pas de Tancat

Follow the narrow channel for 10–15 minutes until you reach the first abseil.

1	3m	This first abseil is very short, or it can be down-climbed with care.
2	3m	Next comes a slightly steeper abseil, but again quite short.
3	6m	A longer abseil follows. Beware this is severely undercut in the upper section.
4	17m	The next abseil ends in a confined chamber.

From here a fixed rope may be in place to help with the exposed scramble out of the marmite to the next abseil.

5	30m	This next abseil is free-hanging.

A scramble down leads to a widening over the riverbed and easy ground for a while. Follow the main canyon downstream to reach the next anchors.

6	5m	A short abseil leads to the 'tube' feature.

7	15m	Abseil down the tube to a double-bolt belay at a hanging stance on the left.

8	25m	Arrange another, steeper abseil from here to continue into the cavern below. (Note: Abseils 7 and 8 can comfortably be combined with an 80m rope.)

The scenery here is quite incredible; stay awhile and savour it.

9	15m	From high anchors on the right wall follow a slightly confined abseil to a spacious landing.

10	4m	A short abseil.

11	12m	The final abseil emerges into the final chamber.

A fixed rope may be in place (February 2020) to aid a scramble out of the marmite.

Return

Once the final difficulties of the canyon are past, walk along the vegetated riverbed until you reach the road by the **green bridge**.

Descending the lower section of the Barranco del Pas de Tancat

ROUTE 22
Barranco del Infierno

Start/finish	Fleix, Vall de Laguar, ///swipes.distributed.forwarded
Grade	V4
Time	Total time 6hr: approach 2hr; route 3hr; return 1hr
Length	1km
Equipment	Harness, helmet, abseil device and prussic, 30m rope, 1 x 120cm sling

A truly spectacular journey, penetrating deep into the mountains. Surrounded by 100m-high smooth limestone cliffs on both sides for much of the journey, there is a big sense of adventure and drama from start to finish. Although the approach walk is long, it is also rather wonderful and worth doing for its own sake.

Access and parking

From the village of Orba take the CV-718 towards Fontilles and Campell. Drive through the narrow high street of Campell and continue for three or four minutes to reach the village of Fleix. There is a large parking area opposite the school on the edge of the village.

Approach

Continue on foot along the Benimaurell road, turning right after about 100m at the PR-CV 147 and go downhill, passing the wash-house/Font Grossa. Shortly after this, turn right onto a path descending towards Juvees d' En Mig. The path is rocky but stepped and well maintained.

Soon you'll reach the **forat** (hole in the rock). Go through this to gain dramatic views over the valley below. Zigzag downwards, crossing a riverbed and continue all the way to the large riverbed at the bottom of the valley. This is the exit from Barranco del Infierno.

Go straight across the riverbed, following the yellow and white paint markings onto a path zigzagging up the terraced hillside. This side of the valley is likely

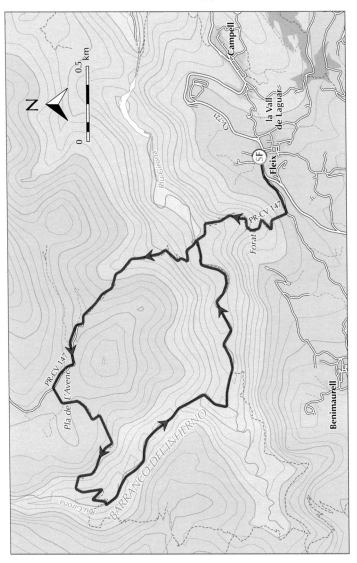

117

to be in the sun and much warmer. When the terrain begins to level out, look out for a small dwelling on the left, where straight ahead is a well. Turn right here, then immediately left onto a surfaced lane, and follow this uphill. Bear right at the crest and descend, passing an old dwelling. After the next house on the left, turn left at the PR-CV 147 sign for Juvees de d'Alt. This soon reaches the large open area of **Pla de L'Avenc**. Signs for Font d' Reinos and Barranco del Infierno are prominently displayed. There is even a topo for the *barranco* (canyon).

A footpath leads toward Barranco del Infierno, soon passing through almond groves before descending more steeply to Font d' Reinos (spring water) and continuing down to the riverbed. Go left along the riverbed to reach the entrance for **Barranco del Infierno** and the first abseil.

The canyon

The abseils are mostly quite short, the longest being around 12m, but there are a lot of them, 10 in total, and a few of the early ones are slightly overhanging. The canyon is well equipped with bolts.

There are a couple of 'via ferrata'-style sections, equipped with fixed ropes (2022). Being traverses, a 120cm sling works well to protect these sections. Mixed in with this and the abseils, is a lot of fun scrambling over smooth, water-worn limestone.

Wrapped up on a chilly December day in Barranco del Infierno

		Barranco del Infierno
1	6m	This kicks off the adventure. A slightly awkward stance that will likely lead to a slight swing on take off.
2	8m	Immediately undercut. Leads to a big ledge; keep going beyond this.
3	2m	A tiny one.
4	3m	Only slightly bigger, but the scenery is getting increasingly interesting.
5	7m	Severely undercut and can give a bit of a swing.
6	3m	Another short one. Leads to some entertaining traversing.

There is an optional traverse along the fixed ropes. This is useful if the pool has water in it. Check fixed ropes prior to use.

7	12m	Into the grand marmite (open pot hole) or, if you're feeling strong, traverse along the fixed ropes, via-ferrata style!
8	3m	Short but awkward.
9	4m	Leads on to the fixed-rope traverse.

Fixed ropes traverse above pools and lead to the final abseil.

10	10m	There are metal staples here.

From here scramble around the pools and through the rock arch to reach a large over-hanging area of rock on the right. This is the end of the technical section.

Return

Continue along the riverbed, bearing leftwards at a confluence, and carry on downstream along the boulder-strewn riverbed, with giant oleander often barring the way ahead, but never a problem. The terrain eases over time, and after about 30 minutes the outward path can be regained at the crossroads. Ascend this back to **Fleix**. About one hour in total.

ROUTE 23

Barranco dels Llidoners and Barranco de Racons

Start/finish	Benimaurell, Vall de Laguar, ///envies.leaving.wiped
Grade	V5
Time	Total time 5hr 10min: approach 10min; route 3hr 30min; return 1hr 30min
Length	1.5km
Equipment	Harness, helmet, abseil device and prussic, 2 x 50m ropes, 1 x 120cm sling

The main event is two massive, airy abseils into dramatic cirques. It's almost certain to be near silent, with beautiful and captivating views over the surrounding canyons. The short riverbed sections provide a real sense of Robinson Crusoe-style adventure and exploration.

Access and parking

From the village of Orba take the CV-718 towards Fontilles and Campell. Drive through the narrow high street of Campell and continue for three or four minutes to reach the village of Fleix, then continue for another 2km beyond Fleix to reach Benimaurell. Park in the large car park next to Bar Oasis.

Approach

Continue on foot going uphill along the road, following signs for PR-CV 147 out of the village, and initially towards the right end of the prominent Caval Verd ridge towering above.

After about five minutes, and just before a small house, reach an information panel showing details for the **Barranco dels Llidoners**. Turn right here to descend steeply on a concrete track. This soon peters out but continue along the stream bed for a few metres until you reach the first abseil.

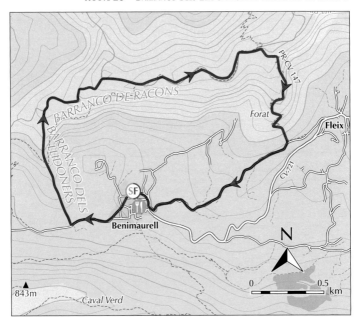

The canyon

Barranco dels Llidoners and Barranco de Racons

1	15m	A double-bolt abseil, over the smooth, easy-angled slab, needs to trend left to a hanging stance accommodating a maximum of three people.

2	45m	From the hanging stance, a triple-bolt abseil reaches the base of this huge cirque. Most of this abseil is free-hanging and through spectacular rock architecture.

Take a vegetated path on the right (looking out) through boulders. This has some easy scrambling, and it passes through a small cave formed by giant boulders.

3	5m	The next abseil is from a small pine tree on the left. Descend a smooth scoop – or with care it is possible to down-climb.

A tricky down-scramble leads to a double-bolt belay.

4	50m	From the double-bolt belay a long abseil, first down steep slabs, and then free-hanging, leads into the second huge cirque.

Follow the small path to a junction, and continue straight ahead, staying with the river-bed. It is now quite overgrown but offers good scrambling for a few hundred metres to a single-bolt abseil.

5	12m	Abseil (single-bolt anchor on right) into a small marmite (open pot hole). Scramble out of this and continue until you soon reach another abseil.
6	12m	From good in-situ thread anchors abseil 12m.

This is the end of the Barranco dels Llidoners, and where the **Barranco de Racons** begins. Turn right and go downstream. Tackle a tricky step from its left side and another tricky step more directly.

7	2m	A short abseil (thread), or an exposed scramble down over ledges, leads into a narrow channel with a rock wall on its right side.
8	12m	At the far end of this channel is an abseil that is quite constricted at first.

More scrambling reaches a wide riverbed.

Return

Continue along the wide riverbed, bearing right at a confluence, and continue downstream along the boulder-strewn riverbed, with giant oleander often blocking your view of the best route. The terrain gradually eases, and after about 30 minutes a path – marked out by yellow and white paint – crosses the riverbed. Turn right here to zigzag uphill, passing through a **forat** (natural hole in the rock), to reach a minor road below the village of Fleix. Here a sign shows the way back to Benimaurell. Follow this to reach **Benimaurell** in around 1.3km.

Huge abseils characterise the Barranco dels Llidoners

🌐 ROUTE 24
Barranco del Pas de Calvo

Start/finish	Pla de Petracos, Castell de Castells, ///harpoon.goody. contrasted
Grade	V3
Time	Total time 2hr 30min: approach 20min; route 2hr; return 10min
Length	500m
Equipment	Harness, helmet, abseil device and prussic, 50m rope

An easily accessible canyon in a beautiful setting. This, the best of the shorter canyons, manages to have a big feel to it. A distinct sensation of wilderness oozes from every crevice. Keep a lookout for wild animals, and look up when the ravens start to call, the sky can fill with them. For more distraction, combine this with a walk along the Malafí riverbed – PR-CV 168, or explore the quaint village of Castell de Castells.

Access and parking

From the N-332 coast road, turn onto the CV-750 towards Jalón/Xaló and continue through this town to reach Alcalalí and turn left onto the CV-720. Follow this to Parcent and then towards Castell de Castells. About 4km before Castell de Castells, turn right at Villa Mercedes, following signs for Pla de Petracos. Drive on this good single-track road for 3.5km, passing Pla de Petracos (ancient cave paintings here) after 1.6km. Park in a lay-by next to the wide riverbed just before a signpost for the PR-CV 168. There are imposing cliffs straight ahead.

Approach

From the lay-by continue on foot across the riverbed and onto a track leading to an olive grove. Go diagonally through the olive grove, taking extra care if harvesting is taking place. Emerge on the uphill side of the olive grove below steeper ground and look out for yellow and green paint markings. Follow the paint and

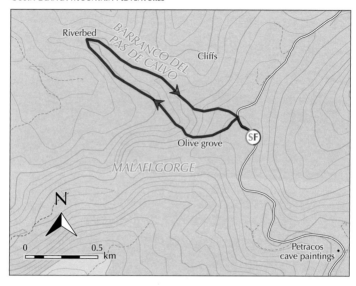

cairns through scrub, and on a vague path heading towards the right-hand end of crags that are on the left side of a *barranco* (canyon). Scramble over low rocks on the right, then traverse above the *barranco*, until you reach the riverbed at the top of the *barranco*.

The canyon

Barranco del Pas de Calvo		
1	23m	The first abseil is from bolts located high up on the right. (There are more bolts on the very edge; don't be tempted!) This descends to a narrow slot leading straight to the following abseil.
2	3m	From a single bolt down easy terrain.
3	17m	Almost immediately another single-bolt belay can be found on the left. This abseil begins steep and awkward, then has a level mid-section, before an awkward finish. There is a huge sloping ledge part-way down; keep going to descend the steep groove to the bottom.

| 4 | 10m | Shortly, you'll reach a double-bolt belay. Abseil to a more open area. This abseil is slightly overhanging. |

Scrambling leads to a very short abseil or down-climb.

| 5 | 2m | A very short abseil from a single bolt, or scramble down this for added entertainment. |

A little more scrambling leads to the final abseil.

| 6 | 5m | A short abseil to finish. |

Return

After the final abseil, continue along the riverbed to reach almond groves and the road.

ROUTE 25

 Barranco del Parent

Start/finish	Alhama Springs, Altea la Vella, ///insurance.dowries.whispering
Grade	V4
Time	Total time 3hr 40min: approach 40min; route 2hr 30min; return 30min
Length	700m
Equipment	Harness, helmet, abseil device and prussic, 80m rope

An open canyon with outstanding views down to the coast and Sierra Helada. It has a sunny and sheltered aspect so expect it to be warm/hot. There are lots of short scrambles during the descent, mostly straightforward and all fun. All abseil stations are equipped (February 2019) with either single or double bolts, apart from a couple that have in-situ rope around trees.

Access and parking

From Calpe and the N-332, turn onto the CV-755 which soon passes through the town of Altea la Vella. Once through the town, look out for a turning on the right, signposted for Alhama Springs. Turn onto this minor road leading through the *urbanización* to Calle Colina and a roundabout. Go left at the roundabout, then take a right turn with a 'no through road' sign, and park at end of this lane. This is also Calle Colina. Note: with a 4x4 it is possible to drive further along the track to park next to a **green building**.

Approach

Continue on foot, turning right just before a **small round tower** and the green building. Follow the good path zigzagging uphill for about 30 minutes. When the steepness eases, look out for a vague path leading off rightwards. Follow this, descending gently through scrub, to reach the head of the *barranco* (canyon).

The canyon

Barranco del Parent		
1	12m	An airy start. This often has a fixed rope in place to help you access the abseil anchors.
2	5m	Short and open.
3	5m	Fixed cord around pine tree.
4	5m	Another short descent.
5	6m	Slightly longer and more awkward, but leads to an open aspect.

Before the next abseil there is a nice lunch spot with beautiful views and a small cave to the right.

6	12m	Fixed cord around pine tree.
7	18m	A fine grey wall of layered limestone.

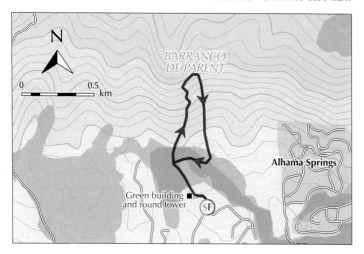

8   40m   This goes all the way to the small pools far below. Don't be tempted to pull the ropes after arriving in the first marmite (open pot hole)! Keep going all the way to the bottom. There is often water in the pools here, but they are easily avoided.

Return
From the final abseil, continue to scramble along the riverbed for about 100m until it is possible to exit onto a vague track on the right. This is loose and requires care, but soon you'll reach the good and well-maintained outbound path.

ROUTE 26
Barranco de l'Estret de Cardos

Start/finish	Pinós, Bernia, ///bystanders.prequel.observatory
Grade	V3
Time	Total time 3hr: approach 15min; route 2hr; return 45min
Length	1km
Equipment	40m rope
Notes	From 1 January to 30 June there is no access to the canyon and surroundings. This is because of nesting birds, so please respect this. There is usually a notice in place. The optimum time to visit is from October to December. Although this is normally a dry canyon, heavy or prolonged rainfall will cause the marmites (open pot holes) to fill up making this a far more difficult, and colder, experience.

A short trip in a dramatic setting below the Bernia ridge. Despite being close to the motorway, the canyon remains isolated and almost silent, with wildlife providing any soundtrack. Impressive scenery and mostly short abseils mixed with fun scrambling make this a great short day out.

Access and parking

From the N-332 between Calpe and Benissa, take the turning for Xaló/Jalón and Alcalalí, then almost immediately turn left again onto the Pinós road. Shortly after passing through the village of Pinós, look out for the 19km marker post and Virgin Mary cross. Turn left here and follow the lower, right-hand fork of this small lane. Continue along here to the valley bottom and park in one of the small lay-bys.

Approach

From the parking area you will see a large gash in the side of the mountain. This is the canyon.

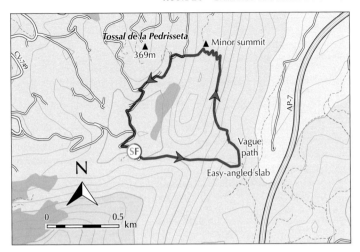

Follow the small track along the riverbed, passing some impressive caves along the way. After around 15 minutes of walking and easy scrambling along the riverbed, the first abseil will be reached.

The canyon

Barranco de l'Estret de Cardos

1	15m	A short diagonal abseil leads to a small ledge and another abseil station. Here it is possible to just clip the ropes through the big snapgate carabiner and continue the abseil. (Some, though, may prefer to rig another abseil from here.) There are three bolts with hangers on the ledge, making it easy to stay safe if rigging another abseil. Continue diagonally left, keeping out of the deep marmite. It looks much further left to the ledge, but thankfully some of the ledge is out of sight and is easy to reach.

Within a few metres, the next abseil station will appear. Here, there are two options. The second option is trickier and more fun.

2a	2m	Make a very short abseil from the single bolt.
2b	5m	Use the in-situ fixed rope on the right to make a traverse along the right wall of the canyon until you reach an abseil station after about 8m. This leads to a 5m abseil.

3	5m	Immediately after, comes another 5m abseil.
4	17m	A longer abseil leads into a huge marmite ahead.

A grab rope on the far side of the marmite can be used to ease the climb back out. Without using the fixed rope, there are a few moves of about 4+ (French climbing grade). For anyone unsure, it would be well worth using the rope. Look out for the easy-angled slabs soon after this final climb.

Return

The return route is straightforward and on good paths, with views of the Sierra de Oltá and the coast.

The canyon soon opens up and you descend a wide, **easy-angled slab** of rough limestone to reach the open riverbed once more. Almost immediately after this, the number '1' is painted on a rock, with a cairn next to it. Go left here (looking downstream) on a **vague path** leading uphill out of the canyon. Look out for small blobs of red paint and follow these. Soon you will reach a good path. Turn left onto this and follow the zigzags to the top of the hill. Descend the other side, still on the same path, which turns into a wide track. Go left just before you reach a house (noisy dogs) on a dirt track. Soon a small path forks off to the left, taking you back to the road. Go downhill to reach the parking area.

Exiting the main chamber in Barranco l'Estret de Cardos will sometimes require a back-up rope

ROUTE 27

Barranco de Mascarat

Start/finish	N-332 Mascarat road tunnels, Calpe, ///anteater.variably. minded
Grade	V3
Time	Total time 1hr 35min: approach 5min; route 1hr; return 30min
Length	500m
Equipment	Harness, helmet, abseil device and prussic, 50m rope

A short outing in an unlikely setting. Road and rail bridges tower high above, dominating the atmosphere towards the end of the trip, but overall they are surprisingly unintrusive. Once past the first abseil, the walls of the canyon close in and rise to give seriously impressive rock architecture, complete with giant jammed boulders.

It is worth saving this one for a sunny day when the dramatic light effect will be quite a treat.

The canyon was equipped during autumn 2020.

Access and parking

From the north, follow the N-332 until just beyond Calpe, then look out for a turning into the Urbanización Maryvilla. About 150m after this, you will reach a lay-by on the right. This is immediately prior to reaching the first of the Mascarat road tunnels.

Park in the lay-by on the N-332.

Approach

Walk towards the first tunnel. A few metres before entering the tunnel, cross over the crash barriers to access a steep scree slope, with a vague path picking a route to its base. Abseil or clamber down the scree into the riverbed and go downstream to reach the top of the canyon.

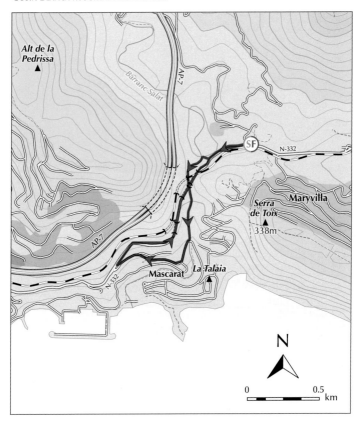

The canyon

Barranco de Mascarat

You'll come to a short, single-bolt abseil station at the entrance to the canyon, but this can be by-passed via a scramble on the right.

1	7m	The first obligatory abseil is from twin bolts on the right to reach a bowl. The next abseil can be seen from this point.

| 2 | 8m | It is possible to arrange a Tyrolean traverse or guided abseil descent here – useful if there is water in the pool. |

Then boulder-hop over the pool. Or, using the extra bolt in the right wall, go diagonally across the wall to clear the pool. Using that extra bolt is arguably more fun, but a splash in the pool becomes more likely. A guided abseil can be set up for those following.

| 3 | 6m | This abseil leads to a dramatic narrowing and the final abseil. |

| 4 | 20m | The final and longer abseil to below the jammed boulders becomes narrow. |

Return
After that final abseil, continue along the narrow riverbed and under the bridges, until you reach the road. Turn right onto the road and follow this uphill through the **Urbanización Mascarat** to reach the **N-332**. Go right at the main road, and follow it through two tunnels to reach the parking lay-by.

Hope the boulder stays put! Barranco de Mascarat

ROUTE 28

Barranco del Curt o Pas de Bandolers

Start/finish	Port de Bernia, CV-749, Jalón, ///exploit.temerity.samba
Grade	V4
Time	Total time 5hr: approach 30min; route 3hr; return 1hr 30min
Length	1km (including some initial walking)
Equipment	Harness, helmet, abseil device and prussic, 2 x 50m ropes

When faced with the Bernia and Ferrer Ridges at close quarters and a mountain panorama filling the middle distance, it would be easy to miss this hidden gem. An easy approach into a tranquil yet dramatic setting sets the stage for a memorable journey that gives not only a canyon descent but some good scrambling on the return leg, for which good route-finding skills will be useful.

Access and parking

From the N-332 near Benissa, turn onto the CV-750 in the direction of Jalón/Xaló. Immediately before entering Jalón, and just after the police station, there is a petrol station on the left. Turn left here onto a smaller road. Follow this until you reach the CV-749 Bernia road, and turn left onto this. Soon the road narrows to single track. Continue for about 10km to a small lay-by immediately before reaching the 11km marker. Park here – or in one of the other small lay-bys nearby.

Approach

Walk back along the road to the **Port de Bernia** sign and, after a few metres, take the minor track left that runs initially parallel to the road. Follow this for a few metres to a left turn onto a path next to a small animal enclosure. Look for some red dots and follow these to descend slightly right on a vague path that zigzags down into the *barranco* (canyon), passing a large **orange crag** on the left. Try not

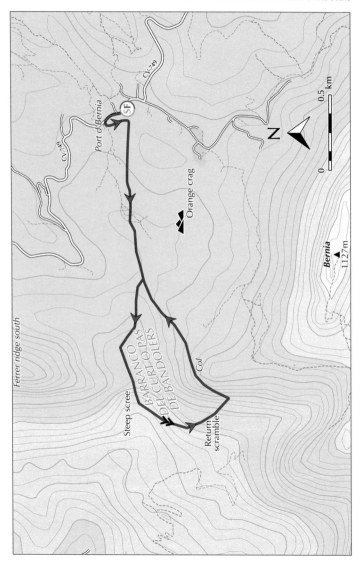

Barranco del Curt o
Pas de Bandolers

Chain and metal steps

Return scramble exits left from steep scree

to deviate from this path until you're in the *barranco*, then stay as close to the riverbed as possible. Occasionally it will be necessary to use the right side of the ravine to avoid the sharp vegetation. You will soon reach the first abseil.

The canyon

Barranco del Curt o Pas de Bandolers		
Once in the barranco, walk about 500m on the right-hand side, picking up and following more red and green dots.		
1	12m	The first abseil is in a dramatic V-groove and reaches a large ledge.
2	23m	Leads into a tricky-to-exit marmite (open pot hole). Combined tactics might help.
3	10m	Drops down to a small but comfortable stance at the next abseil station.
4	36m	A longer abseil in dramatic surroundings leads to a good perch at the next abseil station. The abseil soon becomes free-hanging.
5	45m	To the base of the canyon, free-hanging towards the bottom.

After a short scramble out you'll reach open ground with steep scree slopes on each side.

Return

Go left (looking out) up the steep, rather unpleasant, scree – which thankfully doesn't last long. Consider keeping helmets on.

After about 200–300m notice the large pine tree to the left. Then look for red blobs on the left wall just beyond this pine. Scramble up, following the red and green paint, to a **chain** leading into a gully. Go up the gully– a few **metal steps** mark the way – passing another large pine and at the top go slightly left to reach a **col**. A

Descending the Barranco del Curt o Pas o Bandolers

In the Barranco del Curt o Pas de Bandolers

vague path trends right on a slightly descending traverse line. This leads back into the *barranco*. Cross this by the red arrow, and go upstream, following red/green paint marks. Pass two big crags, exiting the riverbed on the left shortly after the second crag, and following a vague path with more red blobs. A large orange crag is straight ahead, always keep left of this.

Ascend to reach a plateau, and bear left following red paint into pine woodland and back to road.

SPORT CLIMBING

Setting off up Catharsis Somital at Ambolo (Route 34)

✹ SPORT CLIMBING

Costa Blanca is the premier winter destination for Euro sport climbing, with thousands of well-bolted climbs on beautifully sculpted limestone, typically in stunning settings and with easy access. There is little wonder the region has been popular for so long and continues to attract new climbers year on year.

All the crags featured here have easy access and are in sunny settings, ideal for winter visitors. The routes on Candelabra del Sol require an abseil approach, this is described in the text.

The coastal strip from Altea to Denia is the best place to be based for sport climbing on the crags featured here. There is a main road and free motorway running along the coastline and these enable quick access.

Plenty of new routes have been discovered on the Costa Blanca, so expect to find more than are featured here or in any other guide. Both Alcalalí and Toix crags are being further developed as I write.

Around 15 quickdraws are enough for most routes; the number is specified for each crag. For those coming from a trad background it is okay to use your regular quickdraws on an occasional basis for sport climbing, but best not to make a habit of it. They will wear out much more readily when clipping bolts. Many trad quickdraws come with a hooked nose on the karabiner, this is also not ideal for sport climbing. Far better to have a clean nose as this makes for easier clipping and stripping the route afterwards. If you are planning more regular sport-climbing trips it is worth investing in a dedicated set of sport quickdraws with chunky 'dogbone' connectors and clean nose gates.

Grading
Climbs in this section have been graded according to the French system. See Appendix E for a comparison table of climbing grades.

ROUTE 29

Alcalalí

Start point	Parking area, Alcalalí, ///rides.overexposed.integrating
Grade range	3+ to 6a+
Approach time	3min
Aspect/conditions	A southwest-facing suntrap that is often hot even in mid-winter. There are wonderful wide, open views across the Jalón valley, and the road below is quiet, so non-intrusive. The rock dries quickly after rain, although any tufas will seep.
Equipment	60m rope and 14 quickdraws for most of the routes, but routes 1–4 need 70m
Note	Access may be restricted at certain times: please obey any signage.

Although situated by the roadside, the crag is peaceful and the setting is superb, with wonderful views over the olive groves and vineyards of the Jalón valley. Late afternoon is the best time for light, as the sun starts to fall and an orange warmth washes over the rock. Sublime! Busy during weekends and holiday periods.

Access and parking

Take the CV-750 through the town of Jalón/Xaló towards Alcalalí. At the T-junction in Alcalalí turn left then immediately right (signed for Orba/Murla) and follow this for a few hundred yards until a turning on the left leads to a large lay-by set back from the road; park here.

Approach

From the parking area, walk along the road for about 100m to join a small path leading up to the crag.

The crag

1 **Tasha Mítica** 4+, 30m Scramble into the bay then follow the pleasant, jug-laden (plenty of big holds) slab to the top.

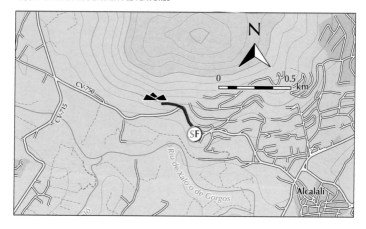

2   **Artmosphere** 6a+, 35m Same start as Tasha Mitica but keep to the right line of bolts, passing an overlap at half height. Tackle the steep wall direct to a spectacular finish through the orange roof.

3   **Rocky** 6a, 35m Climb into the bay between two bushes, climb easy walls to a steepening below a crack. Climb the crack then step right to an orange streak before trending left to the top.

4   **The Baker** 6a+, 35m Start just left of Primero and stay right of the orange scoop then follow the increasingly steep wall to the top. Staying slight right on the headwall is best.

5   **Primero** 3+, 15m Mega jug fest all the way to a large stance. A great first lead.

6   **Ceder o no Ceder** 4-, 15m The next route right gives another jug fest.

7   **Ainee/Aimee** 4+, 16m Start by the hole and make steep moves to yomping. There is a continuation of about 11m to a higher lower-off.

8   **Spare Rib** 4+, 15m Start at the orange rock and make steep moves (tricky for the grade) to reach easier ground.

9   **Rib Eye** 4+, 15m Climb the arête, moving left around the bush. Another good first lead.

10   **Cornered** 4+, 15m 3D climbing leads up the corner stepping right at the bush to reach the bay.

11   **Deep Pockets** 5, 15m Slightly trickier and steeper than its neighbour but with ample deep pockets. Leads to the same bay.

12   **Stolwitter** 6a+, 28m Up the orange streak to the recess. Go direct for the full experience or step slight right for the easier life. Easy moves lead to a lower-off, or continue up the wall above via more interesting moves.

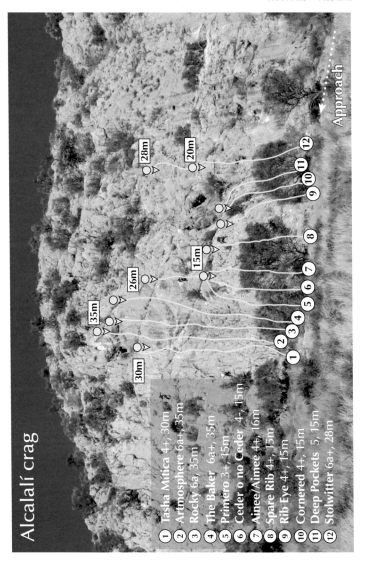

Alcalalí crag

1. Tasha Mitica 4+, 30m
2. Artmosphere 6a+, 35m
3. Rocky 6a, 35m
4. The Baker 6a+, 35m
5. Primero 3+, 15m
6. Ceder o no Ceder 4, 15m
7. Ainee/Aimee 4+, 16m
8. Spare Rib 4+, 15m
9. Rib Eye 4+, 15m
10. Cornered 4+, 15m
11. Deep Pockets 5, 15m
12. Stolwitter 6a+, 28m

ROUTE 30
Los Cerezos

Start point	Lay-by beyond cattle farm off CV-752 between Tarbena and Castell de Castells, ///photographed.shelved.decoys
Grade range	4+ to 6a, with continuation pitches of 6a to 6b
Approach time	The regular walking approach is 15 minutes. Approach via the canyon will take about 1hr.
Aspect/conditions	West-facing – so best around middle of the day. Although this crag nestles in a valley, it is still high up and will be cooler than the coast.
Equipment	60m rope; 14 quickdraws. 80m rope and 20 quickdraws will open up a few more routes here, but are not essential

Set among almond and cherry groves, with superb views and a sheltered setting, this really is a perfect crag. The routes described here are predominantly slab climbs, although the crag does offer much steeper routes on vertical faces. The rock is sharp limestone that has been well bolted. There are three short routes of about 15m, with the remainder being 30m or more. All offer great climbing in a secluded setting. More development of the neighbouring walls is ongoing. Expect company at weekends and holiday periods, otherwise this is a quiet venue.

Access and parking

From the N-332/A-7 coast roads, head towards Callosa d'en Sarrià, then follow signs for Fonts del Algar on the CV-715. This road leads through Bolulla, then winds its way up to Tarbena. Immediately after Tarbena, turn left onto the CV-752 towards Castell de Castells. After about 3km, there is a farm on the right. Then, just after this, turn left and follow the asphalt-surfaced single-track lane until it becomes concrete. Park here in the small lay-by. Please do not park in the olive groves opposite the crag as this may lead to access problems.

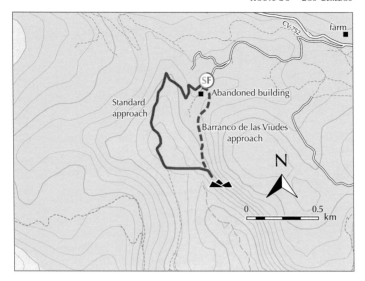

Approach A – the standard approach

Continue on foot along the concrete-surfaced lane and follow this as it descends to reach almond and cherry groves. Follow a small path heading left through the grove to the base of the crag.

Approach B – via Barranco de las Viudes

Walk across the lane to a small path. Follow the path past an abandoned building project, then look out for a small cairn on the left. Descend here a short way to the riverbed and follow this downstream.

Initially the terrain is straightforward, but the scenery keeps things interesting. A few short abseils of less than 5m lead to a 20m abseil. More short abseils continue the descent through the narrowing canyon before the terrain opens out into almond and cherry groves. The crag is on the right. All abseil stations are equipped.

The crag

Routes described left to right. Routes 4–9 have continuation pitches above. All are about 15m and all offer good climbing at only slightly harder grades. An 80m rope is best if doing the continuation pitches, or use the intermediate lower-offs if using a shorter rope. And tie a knot in the end of the rope!

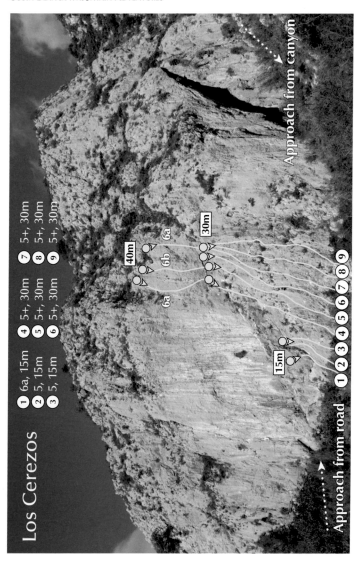

Los Cerezos

1 6a, 15m 4 5+, 30m 7 5+, 30m
2 5, 15m   5 5+, 30m 8 5+, 30m
3 5, 15m   6 5+, 30m 9 5+, 30m

Approach from canyon

Approach from road

1 2 3 4 5 6 7 8 9

40m 6b 6a
6a
30m
15m

1   6a, 15m At the wide clearing below the left end of the crag are three short routes; Route 1 is the left-most of these. Interesting climbing leads to a tricky move at three-quarters height before a few more steep moves reach the chains.

2   5, 15m Starts just right of Route 1 and follows pleasant slabs into a corner leading to a steep wall where the chains are.

3   5, 15m Just right again, this one brushes through some vegetation early on and gives fun moves from the ground. Goes to the same lower-off as the previous route.

4   5+, 30m The first of the longer routes on the big grey slab. Easy climbing leads to a ledge, clip the bolt before making steeper moves, then soon move slightly right to gain big holds and easier ground. Yard up the slab to reach

Los Cerezas offers much steeper routes too!

a steepening, then positive holds lead through the bulges to the upper ledge and the lower-off. Continuation pitch 6a.

5   5+, 30m Another easy start leads to jugs (big holds) and then a delicate diagonal traverse across a slab (going further right to the crack is slightly easier). Jug-pulling leads to another delicate section before you reach the top. Continuation pitch 6b.

6   5+, 30m A steeper start with a few dubious holds but thankfully the bolts are close together. The upper half is

where this route shines, with fine technical climbing on superb limestone. Continuation pitch 6a.

7   5+, 30m Similar to the previous route, although this offers more of a crux sequence, shortly before pulling onto the upper slabs. Continuation pitch 6a.

8   5+, 30m The theme continues with a steeper lower wall leading to pleasant slabs. This one giving some nice delicate moves higher up. Continuation pitch 6a.

9   5+, 30m The final route on this section of wall gives an impressive and sustained pitch. Continuation pitch 6a.

 ROUTE 31

Sierra de Toix

Start point	Road end beyond Castellet de Calpe, Calpe, ///debacles. evenings.strongholds
Grade range	3+ to 5
Approach time	5min
Aspect/conditions	The crag faces southwest and comes into the sun from late-morning. It then stays in the sun all day. It can be quite breezy so the rock will dry very quickly after rain.
Equipment	60m rope; 14 quickdraws

Very easy access, and enjoys an open outlook over the sea towards Sierra Helada. Views are excellent and include many of the big mountains of the region, as well as the close-by Mascarat gorge. There is a main road and local tramway a few hundred metres away, so expect a little noise. Weekends and holiday periods will be busy. Quiet at other times.

Access and parking

Turn off the N-332 into the Urbanización Maryvilla which lies between Calpe and Altea. Follow signs for Castellet de Calpe and continue beyond here to park at the end of the road. The Toix Oeste crags are visible straight ahead.

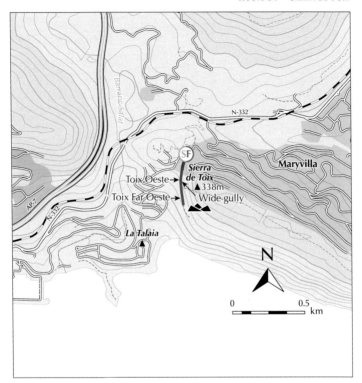

Approach
From the parking area follow the track leading underneath Toix Oeste, then cross a wide gully to reach Toix Far Oeste.

The crag
Routes are described left to right.

1   **Dessie Done Dallas** 3+, 25m First route on the left, with its name painted in green at the base. Very well bolted, makes for a great first lead.
2   **La Roja Una** 3+, 25m The second route on the crag, and just a few feet to the right.
3   **Asombroso** 3+, 20m Climb the face just left of a rib.

149

Toix Far Oeste

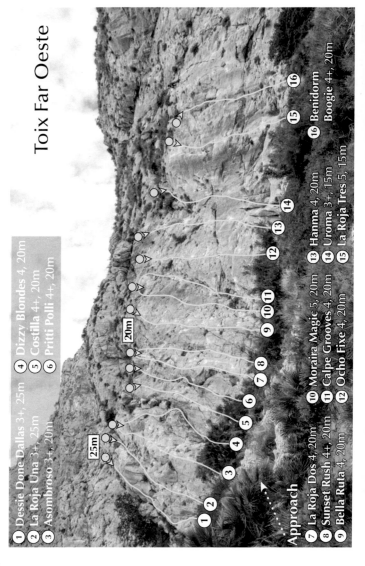

1. Dessie Done Dallas 3+, 25m
2. La Roja Una 3+, 25m
3. Asombroso 3+, 20m
4. Dizzy Blondes 4, 20m
5. Costilla 4+, 20m
6. Pritti Polli 4+, 20m

Approach

7. La Roja Dos 4, 20m
8. Sunset Rush 4+, 20m
9. Bella Ruta 4, 20m
10. Moraira Magic 5, 20m
11. Calpe Grooves 4, 20m
12. Ocho Fixe 4, 20m
13. Hanma 4, 20m
14. Uroma 3+, 15m
15. La Roja Tres 5, 15m
16. Benidorm Boogie 4+, 20m

4   **Dizzy Blondes** 4, 20m Start in a groove just right of the rib and swing left to gain the rib and slab. Name painted in green at the base.

5   **Costilla** 4+, 20m Climb the pleasant slab between the groove and the crack.

6   **Pritti Polli** 4+, 20m 2m right of Costilla. Climb the easy slab to reach a small cave and exit this via a tricky move. A commodious ledge is reached at the top.

7   **La Roja Dos** 4, 20m This route tackles the slab just right of the crack.

8   **Sunset Rush** 4+, 20m Start just right of the previous route and follow the jug-filled slab.

9   **Bella Ruta** 4, 20m More good slab-climbing leading to a leaning corner.

10 **Moraira Magic** 5, 20m Starts about 1m left of Calpe Grooves and tackles the steeper wall on big holds all the way.

11 **Calpe Grooves** 4, 20m Climb the right-trending groove. Name painted in green at the base.

12 **Ocho Fixe** 4, 20m Tackles the slab just right of the previous route. The name suggests eight bolts in the route.

13 **Hanma** 4, 20m Start at a small rib/pinnacle and climb easy slabs directly. Name painted at the base.

14 **Uroma** 3+, 15m Climb from a bay immediately right of the rib/pinnacle, trending right to the lower-off.

15 **La Roja Tres** 5, 15m Start below the white rock and climb this steeply.

16 **Benidorm Boogie** 4+, 20m Steep moves into the orange groove and follow this to a lower-off on the left. Name painted in green at the base.

ROUTE 32
Candelabra del Sol

Start point	Road end beyond Castellet de Calpe, Calpe, ///debacles. evenings.strongholds
Grade range	Magical Mystery Tour 5; Erikindia 6a+; Parle 6a+. All routes are multi-pitch
Approach time	30min
Aspect/conditions	A southwest-facing suntrap. The rock may feel greasy in the morning. Parle offers some shade, the other routes offer no shade.
Equipment	60m abseil rope to leave in-situ. 50m rope for the climbs

All of these climbs cover terrain that is improbable at the grade. Magical Mystery Tour is indeed a fitting name. These are very committing venues with no easy escape should things not go to plan. Let someone know where you are. Despite initial appearances, the rock is surprisingly solid, and with just enough bolts to keep things safe while retaining plenty of adventure. These are classic routes so expect company at weekends.

Access and parking

Same as for Route 31. Turn off the N-332 into the Urbanización Maryvilla, which lies between Calpe and Altea. Follow signs for Castellet de Calpe, continue beyond here to park at the end of the road. The Toix Oeste crags are clearly visible straight ahead.

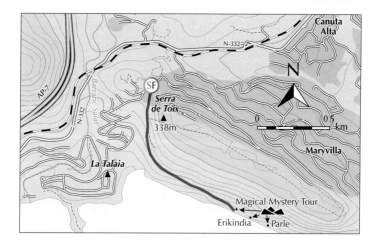

Approach

From the parking area follow a wide track leading below Toix Oeste and stay on this gently descending path as it passes below Toix Far Oeste and continues towards the sea. Small cairns mark the onward route, take care to stick with them. A few minutes after crossing a large gully and descending seaward, you will reach the abseil point for **Magical Mystery Tour**. For **Parle**, follow the narrow path for

Candelabra del Sol - Magical Mystery Tour

Approach

45m

A

5

5

4+

3

2

2+

Candelabra del Sol - Erikindia

Parle

Approach

45m

4+

6a+

5+

Magical mystery tour

five more minutes until you reach a large flat area with two large holes in the ground. The abseil for **Erikindia** is about equidistant between Magical Mystery Tour and Parle. Look out for a small rock window in the ground.

Magical Mystery Tour
Abseil 45m Four unlinked bolts can be equalised.
1) 2+, 25m From the base of the abseil, scramble left (facing in) with care to reach a large thread, belay here. Scramble leftwards (fixed rope may be in place) passing the occasional bolt, into another large cave, traverse around this to reach a bolt on the far side, belay here. Note: this can be backed up with medium wires/cams.
2) 2, 10m More scrambling across gently descending ledges leads to a level platform with a high bolt, belay here.
3) 3, 15m Tackle the steep crack then exit left onto ledges descending to a double-bolt belay.
4) 4+, 20m Traverse left to an arête and make exciting and exposed moves around the corner into a scoop. Continue traversing for a few metres until an overlap can be breached to gain a double-bolt belay in the centre of the scoop.
5) 5, 25m A rising traverse rightwards reaches the arête; climb this to gain increasingly spectacular positions. A few steep moves lead to easier climbing and a small ledge to the right, double-bolt belay.
6) 5, 35m Trend right from the belay, then steeply up on good holds to a hollow, move left here onto an arête. Climb this steeply to sloping ledges, then trend right to gain the groove. Climb this to reach a crack in the right wall and follow this on sharp holds to the top. Double-bolt belay.

Erikindia
Abseil 45m Just left of the rock window is a solitary bolt on flat ground, clip in to this before leaning over the edge to locate a double-bolt abseil station.

1) 5+, 25m From the base of the abseil scramble up a scree-filled gully to locate bolts high on the left wall. Follow these steeply as they trend right, then left, before traversing more steadily leftwards to reach a fabulous stance on an arête.

2) 6a+, 20m Move left to enter the chimney. Bridge up this and soon you'll emerge onto the open face and much steeper ground. The next few moves are quite strenuous but the bolts are reassuringly close. As soon as the terrain eases, go right to a belay station on another fabulous perch.

3) 4+, 25m Follow the depression, aiming for the rock window.

Parle

Abseil 55m Abseil through the first hole, there are bolts well back from the edge. It is possible to re-belay on the edge if desired. It is approximately 55m to the ledge. There is currently no fixed protection at the first stance on Parle, so stay attached to the abseil rope.

1) 5+, 20m Climb the left wall, which is steeper than it appears. Trend rightwards to reach a rock bridge in a stunning position. Double-bolt belay.

2) 6a, 20m Climb the wall directly above the belay, and after a few metres trend slightly left to a groove. Follow this to reach a prominent break and traverse rightwards along this to a hanging stance and double-bolt belay.

3) 6a+, 20m Traverse left, then ascend diagonally towards the light. Savour the positions and atmosphere before exiting through the big hole. A magnificent pitch.

Arriving at the rock bridge belay on Parle

Candelabra del Sol – Parle

A

55m

6a+

6a

5+

ROUTE 33
Morro Falquí

Start point	Calle Fresnos, Benitatxell, ///transparent.winked. vocations
Grade	Silberruecken 6c; Sonjannika 5+ (with optional 6a+ pitch); 95 Olé 6a. All routes are multi-pitch
Time	Total time 4hr 35min: approach 30min; route 4hr; return 5min
Aspect/conditions	Southwest and a sun trap. Can feel very warm here even in mid-winter.
Equipment	50m rope (minimum); 15 quickdraws including a couple of extenders/alpine 'draws. For Sonjannika also take a 60cm/120cm sling for nearby threads

A large, south-facing sea cliff offering excellent climbing on sharp limestone. The three routes described here are the extent of current development on this face. There are also single-pitch routes on the west face, which can be accessed from the top of the crag. Towering above the sea and being south-facing does mean this place gets hot. Thoughtful equipping, superb surroundings and brilliant climbing ensure a great day out. Sonjannika will usually have traffic at weekends. The other routes are currently less popular, but every bit as worthwhile.

Access and parking

From the N-332 just north of Benissa, turn onto the CV-740 towards Teulada, and continue on to Benitatxell. Go straight over the crossroads in the centre of town and at the next set of traffic lights take the right fork towards Cumbre del Sol and Platjes/Playas. After ascending for a few hundred metres you'll reach a fine viewpoint. Drive on and head downhill, past a large school on the right and into the *urbanización*. Continue along this road until you reach a small supermarket. Take the left turning shortly after this. Follow this road to a roundabout and turn right here onto Calle de Cordell Hull. After about

100m the road bears around to the left, where there is a sharp right-hand turning or an option to continue straight ahead. Go straight ahead and follow this lane for a couple of hundred metres. When the road turns sharply to the left, take the right turning onto a 'no through road'. Park considerately along here.

Approach

From the parking area go to the end of the lane to reach a walkers' signpost. Turn right here to follow a small path leading almost immediately right again and descend into woodland. After a few minutes the path emerges via a gate onto a road by a row of garages. Turn left onto the road which soon goes uphill. Opposite a junction is a green blob on the low left-hand wall. Cross the wall here to gain a good path leading into the **Barranco de Testos** (canyon).

Once in the *barranco* follow it towards the sea. This soon involves some scrambling, and you'll encounter two sets of fixed ropes to aid the descent down slippery rocks. Once beyond the second fixed rope, and still a little way above the secluded beach, look out on the left (looking seawards) for a vague path leading under the huge cliffs. Follow this path under impressive overhangs. When the cliff abruptly turns, descend towards the beach on a zigzag path that will turn back towards the cliff after a few metres. Soon you'll see red dots and arrows on the rock. Follow these to your chosen route. From left to right is: Silberruecken, Sonjannika, and 95 Olé.

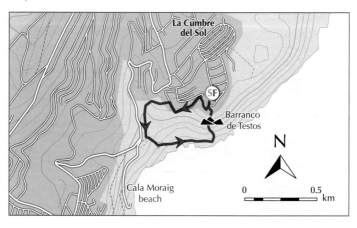

Silberruecken

1) 4+, 35m Start as for Sonjannika, and after a few metres, veer leftwards to go directly up the slab to a good ledge and double-bolt belay.

2) 6c, 30m Climb the crack on the right, then onto a steep face which has thin, delicate moves, before the easier finish up a slab. Double-bolt belay.

3) 6b, 35m Traverse left then back rightwards to the edge of a big cave. Exit this leftwards via more steep moves before a technical slab leads to the double-bolt belay on the big ledge.

Finish up the final 2 pitches of Sonjannika.

Sonjannika

1) 4, 40m From the red dot follow a rising traverse rightwards for the full 40m – to a good stance and double-bolt belay. Take care not to follow the Silberruecken bolts.

2) 5, 15m Head steeply up the prominent groove, then trend left up the wall, to a small stance and double-bolt belay.

3) 5+, 30m Traverse rightwards off the belay, then diagonally rightwards, until a more direct line can be followed up to a fine slab. Traverse leftwards into an airy position on the slab, then more directly until almost level with a small cave on the right. Traverse easily across to this and make an exposed and tricky move into the cave to belay on double bolts. There is usually some shade in the cave.

4) 5, 20m Step out of the cave in a seaward direction and marvel at the fantastic exposure. Continue rightwards to small ledges and a prominent nose. Follow this, direct at first, then trend slightly left to reach a double-bolt belay on the edge of a huge ledge. You now face a choice.

5a) 6a+, 25m Clamber onto the huge boulders at the back of the big ledge and find a double-bolt belay. From here, traverse easily rightwards into a corner. Move steeply up this, step right onto the slab and follow this to a small ledge. Then steeper moves, on wonderfully sharp rock, lead to a big ledge and double-bolt belay.

5b) Grade 2 scramble – Follow a vague path skirting around the left side of the crag. Once clear of the crag, it bends back rightwards and leads to a slab with fixed rope. Climb this easily (beware – the fixed rope rubs on the sharp rock – do not rely on it), then follow ledges rightwards to a double-bolt belay on a large ledge.

6a) 5+, 40m Climb directly up from the belay. A few steep moves lead to an easier mid-section. The shallow groove is tackled direct and, moving right on the glacis, you'll reach a huge block. Move up and traverse back left about 6m to an edge and onto a slab to reach a single-bolt belay set back about 1m from the cliff top.

Morro Falquí

Descent...

Scramble alternative to 6a+ pitch

1 Silberreucken 6c
2 Sonjannika 5+
(optional 6a+ pitch)
3 95 Olé 6a

Approach via canyon

Beach

6b) 6a, 35m A more direct finish is the 'Moorhun Winter Edition'. It starts 5m left of the double-bolt belay. Make steep moves on jugs (big holds) to reach a delicate slab and follow this up to a recess and easier slabs. Finally follow the prominent orange groove – steeply up on glorious holds all the way to the top and the double-bolt belay. Note: it can be very windy on this belay!

95 Olé

1) 4, 30m From the small ledge follow ring bolts easily and directly up the pleasantly angled slab. Move right at the top to a double-bolt belay on a small stance.

2) 5+, 30m Steep climbing up the groove, with some fine bridging positions. From the top of the groove move left onto slabs and cruise up to the double-bolt belay on a good ledge a few metres below the cave of Sonjannika.

The airy third pitch of 95 Olé

3) 6a, 25m Steep and strenuous moves off the belay lead to a rightwards traverse line under a nose. Once on the prominent nose, trend slightly left to a double-bolt belay on the edge of a large ledge.

If you want an easier finish, head up Sonjannika pitches 5 and 6 and you'll keep the grade more in line with the rest of the route. However, for those seeking more adventure and the higher grade of 6b+ read on.

From the large ledge at the top of pitch 3, walk rightwards under roofs, passing a scattering of large blocks, to reach another commodious ledge. Cross this to reach a double-bolt belay.

4) 4+, 24m Climb the slab left to right to reach a sloping ledge, and cross this with caution to a double-bolt belay.

5) 6b+, 45m The impressive and long corner groove provides the meat of this pitch. Beware of friable rock and prepare for steep and strenuous climbing that may promise to relent but doesn't! Double-bolt belay at the top.

🧗 ROUTE 34
Ambolo

Start point	Calle de la Torre Ambolo, near Cap de la Nau, Jávea, /// swoon.swine.feminism
Grade range	4+ to 6a
Approach time	5min
Aspect/conditions	South-facing and comes into sun from about midday. Due to the recessed position of the crag, it can get hot! If it does all get a bit too much, just follow the steps down to the shore. This is a popular swimming spot.
Equipment	For all apart from route 12, a 50m rope will suffice. For route 12 a 70m single is required. 12 quickdraws

The seaside resort of Jávea may be better known for its golden sands, marina and waterfront restaurants. But it offers so much more, including this secluded crag complete with gorgeous views over the Granadella bay. It was developed years ago but has enjoyed a revival recently, with new routes appearing and existing routes being re-bolted. All the climbs described here are on slabs offering superb friction on rough, pocketed limestone. Sun and shade can generally be found, as the buttresses face most directions. This crag can be a good bet when the weather is misbehaving inland. Recent retro-bolting of routes here will likely mean a rise in popularity. But currently this is a quiet venue.

Access and parking

From the N-332 follow signs for Jávea/Xàbia, turn right at a roundabout, follow signs for Benitatxell and then follow brown tourist signs for Cap de la Nau. Immediately before reaching Cap de la Nau, turn right onto Calle de la Torre Ambolo and park at the end of this lane.

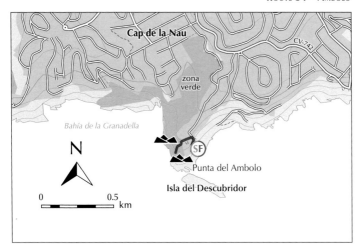

Approach
Opposite a viewpoint and picnic area is a footpath. Follow this to reach steps descending to the crag.

The crag
Routes are described left to right. Some routes have their name painted at the base.

1   **Golden Gate** 5, 22m The lower wall is a little technical and leads to an easy middle section, before the sting in the tail.
2   **Pardillos** 5+, 22m Sharp holds on the lower wall lead to the easy middle section, and another crux right at the top.
3   **Lucas** 6a, 15m More good sport. Start up Angel and climb direct to a shared lower-off with Guiriway.
4   **Angel** 5, 12m This takes a rising-rightwards traverse on jugs (big holds) to reach a double-bolt belay at a recess.
5   **Guiriway** 5+, 14m Start just right of Angel and take a more direct line, keeping left of the recess to finish above the Angel lower-off.
6   **Gwen** 5, 10m Start at the name and climb directly via a series of mega-jugs to the recess.
7   **Achicharra** 4+, 20m About one minute further down the path is another slab. This is the left-most route and the longest on this sector. It trends slightly right to reach a selection of shared belays.

Ambolo upper slabs

1 Golden Gate 5, 22m
2 Pardillos 5+ 22m
3 Lucas 6a, 15m
4 Angel 5, 12m
5 Guiriway 5+ 14m
6 Gwen 5, 10m

Approach path

22m 15m 10m

Ambolo lower slabs

7 **Achicharra** 4+, 20m
8 **Chita a Ciegas** 5, 15m
9 **Rosetta** 5+, 15m
10 **Escàndalo Público** 5, 15m

20m

Ambolo
lower slabs

Chita a Ciegas 5 at Ambolo

8   **Chita a Ciegas** 5, 15m The next route rightwards has a tricky middle section before easy climbing above.

9   **Rosetta** 5+, 15m Some great moves, particularly the technical middle section where it gets a bit thin. Well bolted where it matters.

10 **Escándalo Público** 5, 15m The rightmost route on this buttress. A steep start is worth tackling direct through the bulge. Easier but still satisfying climbing remains.

Anyone looking for a more adventurous excursion, read on!

Continue on the footpath down to the water's edge; gear up and stash bags discreetly here. Going right (looking seaward), scramble along exposed ledges just a few metres above the water line. A couple of sections of fixed rope help mark the way. Traverse about 125m to reach a recessed narrow ledge and the start of Catharsis Somital (11).

•   **Catharsis Somital** 4+/5, 48m This too is fully bolted, the first pitch being 33m, and the second about 15m, with double-bolt belays on each. Descent is by abseil, either a 70m single, or – better – two 40m halves.

ROUTE 35

L'Atzúbia (Adsubia)

Start point	Lay-by off CV-717 beyond Adsubia, ///parachutes.seesaw.tubs
Grade range	5 to 6c
Approach time	15min
Aspect/conditions	Southeast-facing with a commanding position on the hillside, making this a very sunny venue, perfect for cooler days. Not much shelter from any rain but it dries out quickly.
Equipment	50m rope; 10 quickdraws is sufficient for the routes featured here. There are some much longer routes at the crag, and these will require an 80m rope and 15+ quickdraws

A large and impressive crag towering above orange groves and commanding fine views out of the Vall de Gallinera towards the coast, Segaria and the church spires of Pego. There is scope for around 40 routes on this crag; so far only about 15 routes exist and here we include the more amenable offerings – all of which can be found at the extreme left end of the crag. The rock is rough, pocketed and well-featured limestone that offers positive, technical wall climbing with friendly spacing between bolts.

Facing southeast, the crag will stay in the sun until around 4pm during the winter months. A few trees at the base offer some shade. This is a quiet venue offering high-quality routes.

Access and parking

From Pego follow the CV-700 towards L'Atzúbia (Adsubia). Drive through this small village, staying on the CV-700 for just over 1km, then turn right onto the CV-717 at a sign for Forna. Follow this road for about 200m to a lay-by and parking area on the left. (Note – there is also parking available immediately after crossing the river and 50m from the CV-700.)

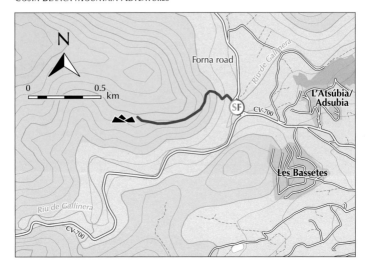

Approach

From the parking area follow a surfaced track uphill, passing a few small buildings on the edge of orange groves. On reaching the end of the surfaced track, go straight on at first then bear left. Look out for cairns and a water channel; turn left into the water channel and walk along this for about 10m. Leave it on the right, onto a good path trending up a rocky clearing in the bushes. Look out for a small cairn marking the start of a small but good path that traverses leftwards toward the rocky skyline. Follow this to the base of the crag.

The crag

Routes are described left to right.

1   **El Tio Canya** 6a, 18m Left-most line of bolts starts just right of a groove. The third clip is tough.

2   **Gervasio García de la Lastra** 5+, 18m Start 2m further right and scramble up the ramp to reach jugs (big holds) leading steeply onto the pocketed wall. Shares lower-off with El Tio Canya.

3   **León Bocanegra** 5+, 18m Starts 2m further right above a date palm. Climb towards the big pocket then follow the pocketed wall into the big corner high up. Finish steeply up the yellow wall.

4   **Harry Potter y la Xina Descomunal** 5+, 18m Another finely pocketed wall leading to steep moves to the same lower-off as León Bocanegra.

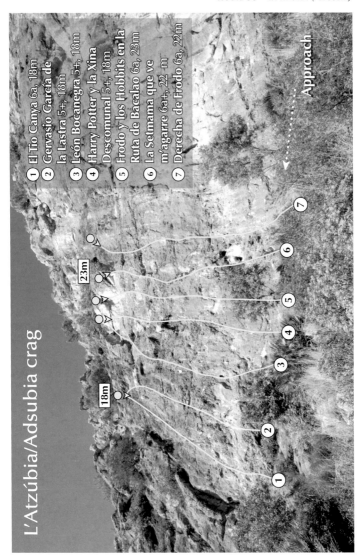

L'Atzúbia/Adsubia crag

1. El Tío Canya 6a, 18m
2. Gervasio García de la Lastra 5+, 18m
3. León Bocanegra 5+, 18m
4. Harry Potter y la Xina Descomunal 5+, 18m
5. Frodo y los Hobbits en'la Ruta de Bacalao 6a, 23m
6. La Setmana que ve m'agarre 6a+, 22 m
7. Derecha de Frodo 6a, 22m

Approach

23m

18m

5 **Frodo y los Hobbits en la Ruta del Bacalao** 6a, 23m From a sapling, fingery slab-climbing (smaller holds and more delicate moves) leads to a sting-in-the-tail finish at the overhang. One bridging move reaches the lower-off.

6 **La Setmana que ve m'agarre** 6a+, 22m Gain the yellow pocketed recess then follow the zigzag crack to a steep finish on the nose.

7 **Derecha de Frodo** 6a, 22m starts just right of the previous route and initially follows a finger-crack (sharp) then an easier wall. Trend right at the top with a trick clip to finish.

Another blue-sky winter's day at Adsubia

ROUTE 36

Sector Cuevas, Cabezón de Oro

Start point	Cueves de Canelobre parking area, Busot, ///leers.depict.raspberry
Grade range	4+ to 6a+
Approach time	5min
Aspect/conditions	South-facing and sunny from about midday.
Equipment	60m rope and 15 quickdraws

By the occasional visitor this is an overlooked mountain, but the locals know better its many fine attributes. When viewed from the A-7 motorway it looks like a big and fairly boring lump of spiky scrub. Once on the Busot road the true scale of the mountain begins to be revealed as does the amount of rock. There are many equipped sport-climbing sectors already developed and no doubt more on the way. Here we describe a sector situated above the popular show caves. It's a relatively recently developed crag which is proving popular. With easy access, far-reaching views and well-bolted routes, it is certainly worth a visit. It's busy at weekends and during local holiday times, but much quieter midweek.

Access and parking

Exit the A-7 at El Campello and follow the CV-773 to Busot. Before arriving in Busot look out for signs for the Cueves de Canelobre and follow these to the parking area immediately below the ridge. If this is full, drive back down the hill for a few hundred metres to a large lay-by and park there.

Approach

Walk past the café to the end of the road where steps lead up to the start of a via ferrata. Continue on the path leading under the crags and above the café to reach the first routes.

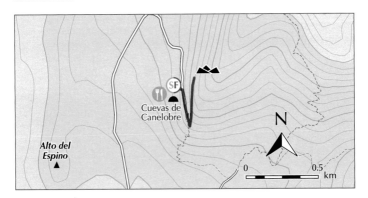

Cabezón d'Oro - (Cabeçó d'Or)

1. La Chunga 4+, 20m
2. El Cambiazo 6a+, 20m
3. Ma Copine 6a, 20m
4. Carla 5+, 30m
5. Las Delicias de Paquito 5+, 30m
6. Mi Pingüina 5+, 30m
7. L'Argilaga 5+, 30m

La Chunga 4+ at Sector Cuevas

The crag

Routes are described right to left. Names and grades are all currently marked at the base of each route.

1   **La Chunga** 4+, 20m The good finger-crack, undercut and layback at half height provide the substance to this one.

2   **El Cambiazo** 6a+, 20m Tough at three-quarters height and a testing pitch at the grade.

3   **Ma Copine** 6a, 20m Good sport and sustained. Still slightly loose low down, but this can be avoided and the route will clean up nicely.

4   **Carla** 5+, 30m Thin and tricky low down then eases to fine jug-pulling.

5   **Las Delicias de Paquito** 5+, 30m A little easier than its neighbour Carla.

6   **Mi Pingüina** 5+, 30m The jug-fest arrives where needed. Another fine pitch.

7   **L'Argilaga** 5+, 30m Sustained slabs give a great pitch at the grade.

TRAD CLIMBING

The involved descent from Aristotles, with the crest in the background (Route 37)

✆ TRAD CLIMBING

Easy but very exposed scrambling marked by occasional cairns on The Edwards Finish (Route 39)

For those looking for more adventure, and who like the big mountain days, there are some stunning mountain routes throughout the region. The iconic Puig Campana is a great place to start, and for mountain routes it is the premier destination in the region, offering routes of nearly 1km in length. The trad is simply fantastic here and routes are usually quiet, except at weekends. There are plenty of other, slightly smaller venues to warm up on too. As with the sport climbing in this area, access is quick and easy, thus allowing early starts without the need for alpine starts.

It is normal to find bolted belay stations and bolted crux sections on the trad routes. In between, a selection of rusty pegs of varying vintage may be found and clipped for that psychological support to back up the trad gear.

During the winter months it is dark at 6pm so allow enough time to complete your objective and get back down. None of the routes featured here are 'Costa clip-ups', they are big mountain adventures, so go prepared and have an amazing time.

Daytime temperatures are often warm enough for just T-shirts, but night-time temperatures in the mountains will often dip below zero.

We recommend using half-ropes as this allows for quicker retreats if required.

Grading
Climbs in this section have been graded according to the UIAA system. See Appendix E for a comparison table of climbing grades.

ROUTE 37

Aristotles and Pepsi Crest,
Puig Campana

Start point	Lay-by opposite helipad beyond Font de Molí, Finestrat, ///treadmills.beatable.filed
Ascent	Aristotles 338m; Pepsi Crest continuation 125m
Grade	Aristotles – V+ (VS); Pepsi Crest continuation – IV (HS)
Time	Total time 7hr: approach 30min; route 5hr; descent 1hr 30min
Aspect/conditions	Faces south so can be hot even during the winter months. This huge mountain crag does attract its own weather though, with cloud and wind not uncommon.
Equipment	2x60m half-ropes and a light trad rack with plenty of slings. If continuing to the Pepsi Crest, it is feasible to climb with a single 60m rope as the abseil from there is shorter.
Abseils	Aristotles involves a 10m and 60m abseil; Pepsi Crest involves a 30m and a 10m abseil

This massive wall of rock has many impressive climbs, mostly following strong natural lines. When travelling north from Alicante it's impossible not to notice and be humbled by this mountain. It's more like an alpine wall than a 'Costa clip-up'. The approach is relatively easy but the route is quite committing, apart from the mid-way ledge. If things are going against you there is a 'bail out' option! For such a big wall, the rock quality is good. Descent is more straightforward than for Espolón Central (Route 38), provided the team is competent and practiced in abseiling. This is the most popular mountain crag in the region, but queues are unlikely. This particular route is usually quieter than the nearby Espolón Central.

The suggested pitch lengths work well. However, it would be easy to vary many of the pitches, so no individual pitch markings are included on the topo.

Access and parking

From the centre of Finestrat follow signs for the 'Font de Molí' (spring water here) and continue beyond the *font*, bearing slightly left, over a green bridge to a lay-by opposite a helipad. Note: Vehicles parked on the helipad will be removed by the authorities.

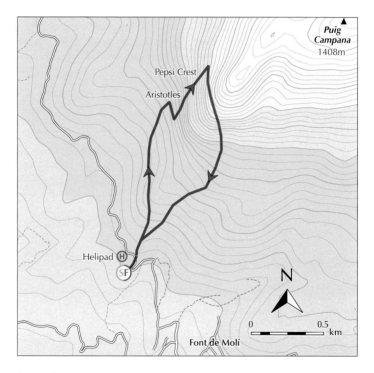

Approach

From the helipad, follow the wide track leading towards the mountain. Ignore the first cairned turning on the right, then, after about 15 minutes, there is another cairned path on the right. Follow this as it forges a route towards the right-hand rib of the huge face of 'Aguja Encantada'. Aristotles can be found at the right-hand side of this face and marked with the word 'Arist' in red paint.

Aristotles and Pepsi Crest

Pepsi Crest

III+ II

IV

Alternative
8a/9a pitches
at V+

Aristotles

III
IV
V+

III
V+ IV
I

Large
ledge

III+ IV+

IV

IV+ IV

III

Approach

Aristotles

1) III, 25m Climb the 'Arist' rib to a block belay.

2) IV, 20m Follow slabs trending right then left to reach a large terrace. The prominent groove harbours a single ring bolt.

3) IV+, 42m Climb the diagonal groove leftwards on satisfying holds. After about 20m the terrain eases and scrambling leads to two white arrows scratched in the rock at a twin-bolt belay.

4) IV, 18m Traverse right over slabs to a large flake, move into a groove with a peg and then threads. Move right again to a thread belay just left of an arête.

5) IV+, 28m Move right to a small bay (peg) and climb the blunt rib with a large recess on the right, to reach a twin-bolt belay below a large slab.

6) III+, 20m Climb directly to a rocky col then move right to gain the **huge ledge**.

7) I, 25m Walk rightwards to the base of a narrow gully with a tree at its top. It is possible to escape from here by scrambling rightwards.

8) IV, 25m Climb the gully for about 10m, then climb more steeply up the left wall to ledges and thread belays.

9) III, 15m Continue up and left to a ledge below a grey slab with a prominent corner. Double-bolt belay.

The alternative is more challenging, some may prefer that, some will prefer easy. It starts at the **huge ledge** at the end of the sixth pitch.

8a) and **9a)** V+, 35m (for those who want a more challenging climb) About 25m left of the gully (see pitch 7) is a fine groove leading to a trio of threaded bolts which can be seen going left to right across the upper wall. Climb the groove before making an airy step right to continue following bolts to reach easier ground and the double-bolt belay below the grey slab.

10) V+, 25m Delicate moves and good footwork lead up the grey slab. Continue to a thread belay on a small stance. An engaging pitch.

The following three pitches can easily be climbed in shorter or longer pitches –natural belays are plentiful. Having said that, the pitch lengths given here do work well.

11) IV, 35m Climb left to a peg before pulling onto the arête. Follow this in sensational positions to a two-bolt belay.

12) IV, 40m Stay on the arête in continually wonderful positions to a thread belay just before the final pinnacle.

13) III, 20m Gain the top of the pinnacle to reach a bolted belay/abseil station.

Descent from Aristotles

Abseil 10m from three bolts and a thread into the prominent notch to reach a good two-bolt belay on the left (looking in). Abseil 60m to reach the gully floor.

Puig Campana south face

Scramble down and left towards a notch. Stay in the gully until below the notch, then cross an exposed but easy rib. Continue descending leftwards to reach the base of a ridge (this is the Espolón Central start). Descend rough tracks towards scrub and pine woodland and go through this on improving paths leading to a plateau. A good path leads back to the road.

Pepsi Crest continuation
This is a natural continuation of the Aristotles line and starts from the prominent notch after the 10m abseil. Allow an extra two to three hours.
1) IV, 35m From the descent notch on Aristotles, climb the wall following in-situ threads. Good climbing for about 20m leads to easy scrambling and a bolted belay on the large ledge.
2) IV, 35m Walk rightwards and descend slightly to a good thread (optional belay), then pass a couple of bolts, continue rightwards with a tricky step by a bolt. Climb up, aiming for the thread up on the arête – climbing this arête is wonderfully airy. A step right into an orange recess leads to a peg over the lip, then easier ground to a bolted belay by a small pine. Rope drag can be a problem on this pitch so consider splitting into two pitches and use the good thread mentioned above.
3) III+, 20m Climb onto an arête and follow this for a few metres until a step down gains a vegetated gully with a larger pine tree.
4) II, 35m Scramble around the left side of the massive pinnacle before trending rightwards to reach its top.

Descent from Pepsi Crest

From the top of the pinnacle descend the rocky ramp, keeping left of the huge gully. The ramp merges with the gully at a col, turn into the gully here and descend with care on the seaward side to reach a double-bolt abseil station on a large slab.

A 30m abseil reaches the gully floor and from here it is possible to scramble with care, or continue the abseil to reach another bolted abseil station on the left wall, it is 70m from the large slab to here. A further abseil of around 10m reaches the ground. Easy scrambling leads to the base of the south face where paths descend to the road.

Note: The gully is home to many trees so care is needed to keep ropes from snagging.

🎯 ROUTE 38
Espolón Central, Puig Campana

Start point	Lay-by opposite helipad beyond Font de Molí, Finestrat, ///treadmills.beatable.filed
Ascent	440m
Grade	V- (HS)
Time	Total time 8hr 10min: approach 40min; 5hr 30min; descent 2hr
Aspect/conditions	Faces south so can be hot even during the winter months. This huge mountain crag does attract its own weather though, with cloud and wind not uncommon.
Equipment	2 x 50m half-ropes are best, but a single 60m is sufficient; a full trad rack with plenty of slings.

The classic 'easy' route on Puig Campana is the most striking as it follows the prominent central pillar, hence the name. For any UK climber operating at HS or above this is a must-do objective. Descents from this route in particular seem to cause more problems than the climbs. If misty, wet or dark, descent will be unpleasant, so plan accordingly. However, on a warm and sunny day the red paint is straightforward enough to follow if you keep eyes peeled.

All the belay ledges are spacious, so if you need to overtake or allow another party to pass, it can easily be done.

Access and parking

From the centre of Finestrat follow signs for the 'Font de Molí' (fresh water here). Continue beyond the *font* bearing slightly left, over a green bridge and to a lay-by opposite a helipad. Note: Vehicles parked on the helipad will be removed by the authorities.

Approach

From the lay-by next to the helipad follow a good track leading towards the mountain, after a few minutes a cairn marks a path on the right, follow this narrow path to reach a short scramble up to a plateau. Continue more easily towards the base of the mountain, aiming for a huge oval shield of rock. The route starts just left of this and is marked by a red arrow and the words 'Esp Central' in faded red paint.

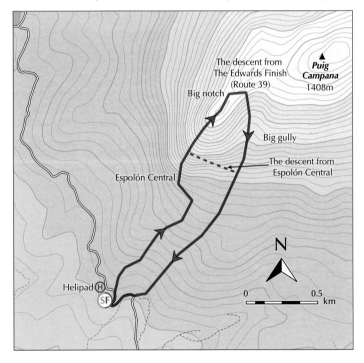

Espolón Central and The Edwards Finish - Puig Campana

Edwards Finish

Descent from top of mountain

Descent from Espolón Central

Top of Espolón Central

Big ledges

Fixed rope

Quick start

Approach

Pitch 10 of Espolón Central

Espolón Central

The quick start If you want to save some time, you can skip pitches 1–3 (below) and instead walk leftwards to the base of the left-to-right arête. Go around the back of this and join it here. Three long pitches of about grade III bring you to the tree belay at the top of the regular pitch 3.

1) IV+, 30m Starting left of the huge shield, follow grooves, ledges and cracks more or less directly to the base of a big corner. At an overlap about 20m up, tackle the central crack. Belay on a good ledge (peg).

2) V, 25m Climb the big groove for 6m, then exit left to continue up the blunt arête to a large ledge and double-bolt belay.

3) IV+, 25m Move slightly right to climb grooves (pegs), passing a tricky move before easier ground and ledges lead to a tree belay.

4) III+, 40m Trend rightwards passing an awkwardly positioned tree, surmount this with interest (it's a bit tricky) and continue up right-trending grooves to **big ledges** and tree belays just before the obvious arête on the right.

5) IV+, 35m Scramble rightwards to the arête and climb this in splendid positions to a peg belay.

6) IV+, 35m Follow a groove and cracks, then the centre of the arête to reach a peg-and-bolt belay on a good ledge.

7) V, 45m Scramble across to the wide chimney/groove and climb this with interest to reach easier ground leading to a **spacious ledge** with a fixed-cable belay on a big tree. This is a good place for lunch and a rest.

8) I, 10m Scramble rightwards to belay on threads below the steeper wall.

9) V, 40m Steep moves up the wall going left at the red arrow then back right to continue up to a two-bolt belay on another good stance on the arête.

10) IV+, 50m Climb into the groove/crack on left side of the arête, follow this to a bolt and thread before making a wild move rightwards to regain the arête in more spectacular positions. Easier climbing leads to a two-bolt belay.

11) IV+, 55m Stay on the arête, taking the line of least resistance. Go to the first big ledge (optional belay and peg) then up either the left or right zigzag crack to another big ledge and two-bolt belay below a large groove.

12) IV, 50m Move into the big groove/chimney and climb this until it opens out and the angle eases. Eventually you will reach the top (tree/block belay).

Descent

At the top of the route look out for a large red blob of faded paint, directly above this is a faded arrow and the word 'GO!' Go right here following the arrow to pass through an improbable-looking gap in the rock. More arrows, red paint and cables mark the way as it traverses across some very steep ground towards a prominent spur. During winter 2020 more cables were added to this line, thus making route-finding easier. After about 20 minutes of traversing, the descent into the main gully will be reached; this is also marked with red paint and has cables to protect the tricky sections. Once in the huge gully, descend this via a vague path on the left. When about level with the base of the crags, look out for a path leading out of the gully on the right (cairns) and follow this through scrub and light pine woodland to traverse back under the base of the mountain and to the plateau leading back to the road.

ROUTE 39

The Edwards Finish, Puig Campana

Start point	Car park at Font de Molí, Finestrat, ///developed.juvenile. isolating
Ascent	563m (200m scramble, 113m climb, 250m scramble)
Grade	V- (VS)
Time	Total time 7hr 30min: approach 2hr; route 3hr 30min; descent 2hr
Aspect/conditions	Faces south so can be hot even during winter. However, it is necessary to go prepared for much cooler conditions higher up on the mountain. This huge mountain crag creates its own weather. Cloud and wind are not uncommon. Navigating off the summit in cloud will be far more challenging and the utmost care will be required to ensure the correct line of descent is taken.
Equipment	A single 50m rope is just sufficient; a full trad rack with plenty of slings; spare clothing; food and water; head torch. Although there are just three climbing pitches, there is a huge amount of very exposed scrambling. Go prepared for a big mountain day.
Abseils	The route involves a 25m abseil
Note	For map, see Route 38.

Climbed as a route in its own right or as a natural extension to Espolón Central, this makes for a great day out in the high mountains. It is a route less travelled so be prepared for trickier route finding and more suspect rock here and there. The route ultimately reaches the prominent notch high on the mountain before tackling a complex descent.

Access and parking

From the centre of Finestrat follow signs for the 'Font de Molí' and park in the large car park here.

Approach

The massive gully to the right of the main rock walls of Puig Campana forms the initial part of this ascent. To gain this, walk along the road for a couple of hundred metres to reach a wide and good track leading uphill, in the general direction of the gully. Take this track and stay with it until you reach the 'Vertical KM' sign. Turn slightly right. This will eventually lead into the gully. Staying on the right-hand side of the gully is easiest as the path is reasonably well formed. About a third of the way up the gully, look out for some large blobs of orange paint on a huge boulder well to the left. Once spotted, aim to reach this boulder via a right-to-left traverse, and then continue traversing, following more orange paint, to reach the start of the approach scramble.

For those wanting a massive day out, an alternative and very satisfying approach to this is to climb Espolón Central to reach this point.

The Edwards Finish

1) II, 200m Scramble over pinnacles and spires to a large pillar with a huge gully on the left. Block belay.

2) III+, 45m Traverse left onto sloping ledges above the dramatic gully. A precarious step gains the gully. Scramble easily up the gully. Just below a huge chockstone there is a very good thread belay on the left wall. Belay here or on small ledges directly below the chockstone.

3) V, 28m Climb the wall trending slightly right, then follow a blunt arête going slightly left, to reach a large ledge with thread belays at ground level. There are

The initial ridge of The Edwards Finish

in-situ threads about 10m right – but to gain these would involve crossing a loose gully, so don't bother.

4) V, 40m Climb the wall direct, aiming for the ridge and passing occasional in-situ threads, to reach more level ground below holm oak trees. Belay on blocks back from the edge.

5) I-II, 250m Easy scrambling and walking will lead to the southeast summit. Stay on the crest for most interest and to keep out of the spiky vegetation. Admire the views before following cairns leading down on the seaward side to reach the big notch.

Descent

Small cairns lead out of the notch on the seaward side. These trend towards the main summit and lead to a double-bolted abseil station at the top of a slab. The abseil is 25m down the slab. Some ancient via ferrata cable runs down the slab and could be used for a down-climb, in extremis!

Traverse across scree following cairns leading towards the main summit and into the gully.

Once in the gully descend back to the roadside as described in the Espolón Central section (Route 38).

🏃 ROUTE 40
Via Gene, Cabezón de Oro

Start point	Lay-by near Cuevas de Canelobre, Busot, ///unwed. decreases.alarming
Ascent	260m
Grade	V (VS)
Time	Total time: 6hr 30min: approach 30min; route 5hr; descent 1hr
Aspect/conditions	Faces southwest and shady until about 1pm during the winter months. This is a big mountain crag which attracts its own weather. In particular, it is often windy.
Equipment	A single 70m rope is enough, although half 50ms would be a better choice. A full trad rack with plenty of slings; medium-sized cams and a few nuts/offsets. Spare clothing, food and water, head torch.
Abseils	The route involves two abseils of 30m and 35m

The Pared de los Alcoyanos face is huge and a mega crag of the Cabezón de Oro mountain range. As well as big trad routes, there is multi-pitch sport and some single-pitch sport climbing available. The mountain even has its own guidebook (available locally in the café next to the caves). Recent years have seen a surge in development here, particularly the bolted single-pitch climbing. Sport climbing is popular too and, with lots of recent development, will no doubt continue to be. However, the big trad routes are less travelled and are likely to be quiet.

Access and parking

Exit the A-7 motorway at El Campello junction and drive into the town. At a roundabout by a fuel station turn right onto the CV-777 and follow this towards Busot. From the outskirts of Busot take the CV-774 following signs for Cuevas de Canelobre. Shortly before arriving at these show caves there is a sweeping right-hand bend in the road. Park here in the large lay-by.

Approach

From the parking area follow the fairly level and wide track for almost 1 mile until you reach a solitary house. Opposite the house is a small track leading up to the base of the crag. The name 'Gene' is scratched on the rock.

Via Gene

The base of the route is easy to find as the name 'Gene' is etched onto the rock and is just left of where the approach path arrives at the crag.

High up on Via Gene

Via Gene, Cabezón d'Oro

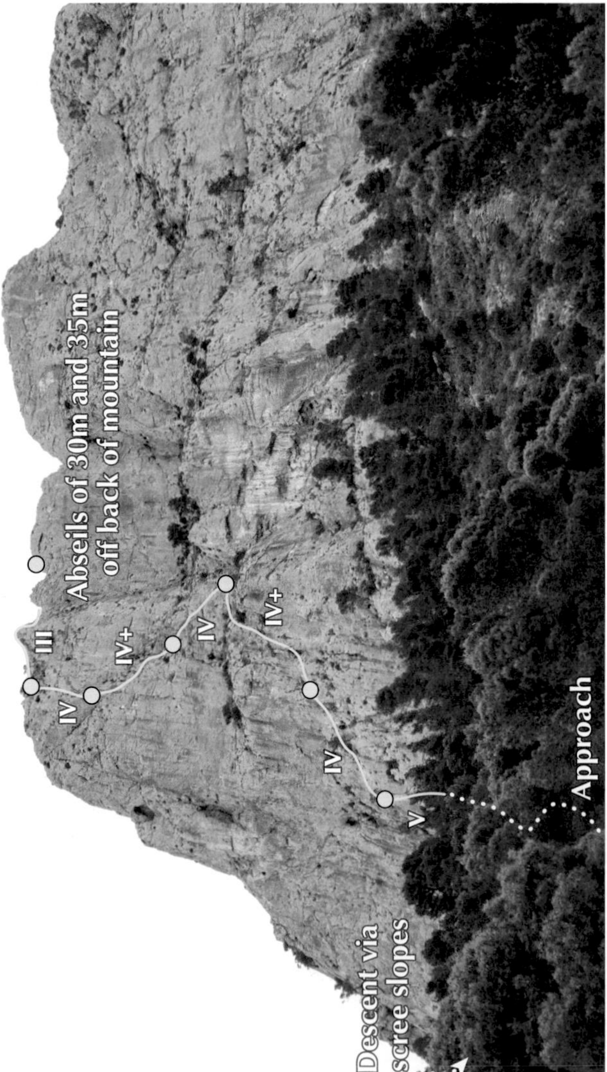

Abseils of 30m and 35m off back of mountain

III

IV+

IV

IV+

IV

IV

V

Approach

Descent via scree slopes

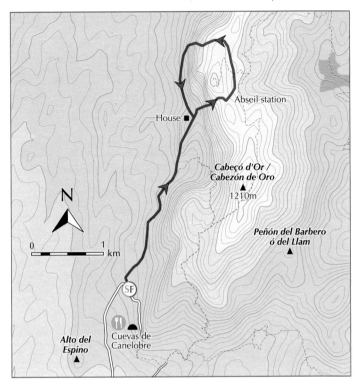

1) V, 30m The first pitch follows the initially vegetated groove-line, before breaking out left to excellent climbing and some of the hardest moves of the day. Belay on the tree next to a small memorial plaque.

2) IV, 35m A rightwards rising traverse passes a tree and a bolted belay on a small stance next to some old pegs. Continue the pitch by climbing a groove on the right until you reach a better stance and double-bolt belay.

3) IV+, 40m Traverse slabs rightwards to a recess with a large bush. Delightful climbing now leads up the pocketed groove above to a huge ledge. Clip the bolt on the edge and continue by scrambling rightwards to belay at the base of a slab. This belay is not equipped.

4) IV, 40m Climb the slab direct, up to a peg, then move right to a thread. Clip this, then trend left to follow the broken rib to a double-bolt belay in a corner.

5) IV+, 35m Go left, passing charred-looking rock under a small tree, until you reach a groove. Climb the groove to a tricky exit left just after a peg and thread. Then continue until you reach a bolt-and-peg belay on a small stance.

6) IV, 35m Continue up the wall, stepping left onto the exposed rib, and follow this to big ledges and a tree belay just below the main ridge.

7) III, 45m Gain the crest and follow it rightwards, taking belays as required. A short down-climb will take you to a notch with bolt belays on either side.

Descent

From the notch, abseiling off the back of the mountain from a bolt belay (2020) is the most straightforward and we recommend this. With either a 70m single or 50m halves, two abseils are needed to reach the scree slopes below. This route is possible with a 60m single rope because there are three abseil stations.

Once on the scree slopes, surf down until it is possible to go left, around to the southwest face and back to the base of the routes.

🥾 ROUTE 41

Arista Agullo, Cabezón de Oro

Start point	Lay-by near Cuevas de Canelobre, Busot, ///unwed.decreases.alarming
Ascent	Mike to supply
Grade	IV+ (HS)
Time	Total time 5hr 10 min: approach 25min; route 4hr; descent 45min
Aspect/conditions	Faces southwest and is shady until about 1pm during the winter months. This is a big mountain crag which attracts its own weather. In particular, it is often windy.
Equipment	50m or 60m single rope is plenty; a light trad rack with plenty of slings; medium-sized cams and a few nuts/offsets

The Peña de Alicante face is huge and one of many mega-crags on the Cabezón de Oro mountain. As well as big trad routes, there is multi-pitch sport and lots of single-pitch sport climbing available. The mountain has its very own guidebook – available locally in the café next to the caves.

Recent years have seen a surge in development here. Peña de Alicante is the showpiece of these crags and any route here will feel big and serious. The sport climbing here is popular and with lots of recent development will no doubt continue to be. However, the big trad routes are less travelled and are likely to be quiet.

Access and parking

Exit the A-7 motorway at the El Campello junction and drive into the town. At a roundabout by a fuel station turn right onto the CV-777 and follow this towards Busot. From the outskirts of Busot take the CV-774 following signs for Cuevas de Canelobre. Shortly before arriving at these show caves there is a sweeping right-hand bend in the road. Park here in the large lay-by.

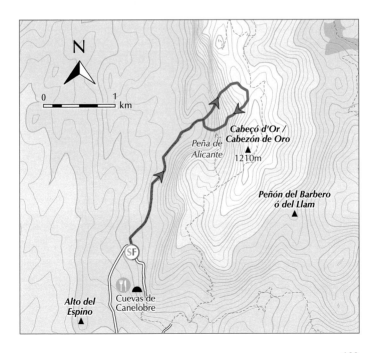

Arista Agullo

Approach

From the parking area follow a wide track going northwest for about 300m (five minutes) to a rise and turn right by a small cairn and signpost onto a path leading towards the riverbed. Follow this good path as it meanders along the riverbed until, after about 10 minutes, it's possible to turn right onto vague tracks leading to the base of a prominent ridge.

Arista Agullo

Start about 25m left of the lowest point, where 'Agullo' is scratched on a slab. Precise and delicate moves lead up the slab with interest. This is a tough start at about grade IV+ with the hardest moves being straight off the ground. You will

soon reach the ridge and easier ground.

There now follows around 100m of grade II, with walking options further right, if time is tight. Some parties may choose to move together/ pitch/solo depending on experience level. Exposure is minimal on the right but soon gathers on the left.

After the introductory scrambling there follow four pitches of climbing, each increasing in difficulty. Occasional fixed pegs and threads mark the way. If in doubt, keep to the crest. There is a bolted belay at

About halfway up Arista Agullo

one stance, and in-situ thread belays at another, but mostly belays need to be constructed.

Grades of the upper pitches are: IV, IV+, IV, IV+, with a distance of approximately 120m over the four pitches.

There is a bolt at the crux move on the final pitch, and plenty of other fixed gear elsewhere on the pitch; alas, this is mostly rather vintage.

Pitches can be split easily with plenty of belay options, hence the lack of description for individual pitches.

Descent

Go rightwards, skirting around the depression and into pine woodland, to meet a good path. Follow this for a few metres until you reach a cairn, then take a vague track rightwards to the summit of **Peña de Alicante**. Continue over this to a steep path leading down to a col. Go right at the col on the steep path down to the base of the mountain.

🚶 ROUTE 42

Via Esther and Scorpion, Vall de Gulabdar

Start point	Parking bay above Guadalest, Vall de Gulabdar, Polop, /// inversions.cornflakes.pilot
Ascent	Scorpion 105m; Via Esther 85m
Grade	Via Esther IV+; Scorpion V (HS/VS)
Approach time	10min
Aspect/conditions	Faces south so can get quite hot even during winter. The base of the crag is quite sheltered, but expect more of a breeze higher up.
Equipment	Half 50ms for Via Esther. A single 60m is sufficient for Scorpion. A full trad rack with plenty of slings; medium-sized cams and a few nuts/offsets. Spare clothing, food and water, head torch
Abseils	Via Esther has 2 x 50m abseils

This large, dome-shaped crag is the first of the big crags as you drive up the valley. There is a huge amount of rock here and lots of good-quality climbing. Almost all of the routes on Paret del Castellet require a full rack, but expect to see a mix of old pegs, in-situ threads and bolts. The base of the crag is fairly flat and open, offering extensive views over to the walls of Ponoch and out to the coast. The crags in this valley are popular, so expect to see other climbers. However, it is the sport climbing that is most popular, so there is a good chance of solitude on these routes.

Access and parking

From the N-332/A-7 coast roads, drive towards the small town of Polop (from the north it is on the CV-715). Upon entering the town from the south, turn right at the roundabout onto the CV-70, signed for Guadalest. Follow this to another roundabout and go straight across and onto a narrow, but surfaced, lane. Soon the tarmac runs out, but only for a short way. At a T-junction, turn right, going uphill and onto a concrete road, then follow this as it rises steeply to reach a small parking bay next to a crag information board. There are more small lay-bys further up the hill if this is already taken.

Approach

From the parking area, continue on foot along the road until the crag comes down to almost meet the road. Follow a small path ascending rightwards under the crags, and pass a sport climbing area before you reach two much larger crags.

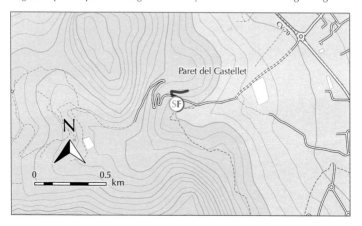

Scorpion, Pared el Castellet

Descent scramble

V+

III+

IV

III

IV+

Scorpion starts at a clearing in a shallow bay. This route is the first to be reached on the approach walk.

Via Esther starts at the right-hand arête of the right-hand crag.

Scorpion

1) IV+, 30m Climb cracks immediately right of the large bush/tree growing a few metres up the crag, and continue up cracks trending slightly left to reach pleasant slabs and a ledge with a bolt belay.

2) III, 20m Move easily across the gentle slab and go between the olive tree (below) and dwarf palm (above), before descending slightly to a single-bolt belay on the arête.

3) IV, 20m Ascend just right of the arête and into a stepped corner leading to a slab. Then head diagonally right up this to a large ledge with two bolts. This pitch could be combined with the following pitch.

4) III+, 10m Move right and climb the short rib, then back left and up to a good ledge below a prominent crack-line. Single-bolt belay.

5) V+, 25m Good moves ascend the crack to reach large hollow-sounding flakes! Traverse left over these, passing a bolt, to reach a fault line below an obvious roof. Tackle the left-trending break steeply until you reach a prominent nose. Pull directly over this, passing to the right of the roof, and reach a bolt/thread belay at the top. An exciting pitch.

Descent

Abseiling back down the line is an option as belays are equipped. However, due to the number of large ledges and bushes, it is probably quicker to walk down. So, from the final belay, walk back from the edge to larger ledges and broken ground. Descend rocky ground, trending rightwards until you reach the road at a sharp bend.

Via Esther

1) IV+, 25m An arête starts at the base of the right-hand edge of the crag, and left edge of a small bay. Scramble up to the base of the arête. Tackle the steep slab from left to right on excellent, but spaced holds. Climb the grooves direct and you will reach easier ground. Then follow corners rightwards to a bolt/thread belay.

2) IV+, 15m Move left from the stance and climb the prominent groove bound on its left by a huge flake. Then soon move onto this and climb to its top, reaching a stance (possible belay) with threads. Continue steeply up the wall on good pockets to reach another stance (no fixed gear).

Via Esther, Pared el Castellet

2 x 50m
abseil

IV

IV+

IV+

IV+

Approach

3) IV+, 25m Go left from the belay and climb the wall via its left edge, then make steep and satisfying moves rightwards to the centre of the wall, and up more easily to a large stance (no fixed gear) on the arête.

4) IV, 20m Step right from the ledge and climb the arête via the left edge and in superb positions. The ground soon eases as you reach the top of the crag. A double-bolt belay can be found on the left.

Descent

From the top of the route, scramble just a few metres to locate a double-bolted abseil station. It is about 100m straight down the face, so you need two abseils. All the abseil stations are fully equipped with double bolts and are on ledges.

It is also possible – and fun – to scramble up to the castle on the summit. The route is obvious. From the castle follow vague tracks downhill, keeping the crag to your left. Once at the road, follow it easily back to the parking area – or back to the crag for another route.

 ROUTE 43

Via Pany, El Peñón de Ifach

Start point	Parking above marina, Calpe, ///tensions.along.reserved
Ascent	212m
Grade	V (VS)
Time	Total time 5hr 25min: approach 25min; route 4hr; return 1hr
Aspect/conditions	El Peñón offers both sun and shade, with most routes being on the south side. This can be hot even in the depths of winter. The north side, which is covered here, offers shade and cooler climbing, and is still ideal for much of the winter. High on the route and during afternoons, more sun will reach this side of the crag.
Equipment	A single 50m rope as a minimum, along with a light rack and plenty of slings
Note	No climbing 1 April–30 June due to nesting birds.

For all that this starts above a large tourist resort and has a friendly feel, it is still a route of over 200m and needs treating with respect. The route featured here is the most popular on the north face and offers excellent quality rock with minimal polish. The north face is the quiet part of the crag so, despite this being the popular route, it still offers peaceful climbing compared to the south side of the crag.

There is so much climbing on El Peñón, it has its very own guidebook! The local climbing shops sell this.

Access and parking

From the N-332 coast road follow signs for Calpe – always aiming for the unmistakable lump of rock sticking 332m out of the sea. Once on the outskirts of the town look out for tourist signs for the Parc Natural del Penyal d'Ifac and follow these to the mariba. There is plenty of on-street parking here.

Approach

Walk back towards the town and take the first turning on the right and go immediately right again. This road soon leads to a wide track that goes to the **Visitor Centre**. Continue on the smaller but still excellent path that leads towards the summit. Follow the path for about 15 minutes until just before the first tunnel. A small path leads off to the right through shrubbery to a clearing in a bay below a prominent chimney. The route starts here.

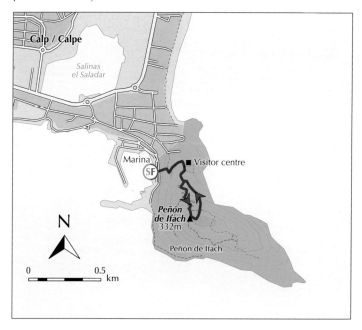

Via Pany -
El Peñón de Ifach

Descent via
tourist path

203

Via Pany

1) IV+, 24m The chimney proves to be awkward but can be well protected. Climb the chimney direct, passing a bulge at half height (bolt). From a small ledge on the left, move rightwards to climb steeper rock (threads) on jugs (big holds) leading to easier ground and a bolted belay.

2) III, 48m Easy climbing and scrambling rightwards along the ramp and through some bushy terrain lead to a final steepening before a spacious ledge. Bolted belay.

3) IV, 35m Ascend directly from the belay, then easier climbing leads into a recess/groove (bolt). Tackle this directly, then move right, before a fine traverse left to reach a bolted belay below a steep chimney.

4) V, 20m Climb the chimney for a few metres until a move right gives more steep moves leading into a corner. Follow this to a good ledge and bolted belay.

5) IV, 25m Step right, going around a corner to reach easy slabs leading rightwards to the top of a buttress and double-bolted belay on a spacious ledge.

6) IV+, 30m Climb directly above the belay and follow a crack, passing a bolt at 7m. Then a few metres more, until moves right cross a slab to a crack to the right of an orange overlap. Climb this steep crack to easy ground and a double-bolt belay on the left.

7) IV+, 30m Steep moves from the belay lead left to easier ground. Keep trending leftwards to a groove and follow this to a bolted belay just below the summit trig point.

Descent

Follow the well-marked, rocky and exceedingly slippery path descending back to Calpe. There are plenty of seaside bars and restaurants near the marina that are worth visiting for post-climb refreshments.

HIKING

Walkers on the south side of Bernia ridge (Route 47)

🚶 HIKING

Here we are including some of the lesser-known routes as well as different takes on more popular outings. All are on predominantly good paths that have waymarking. Winter is the optimum time to be exploring the mountains of the Costa Blanca. During February the valleys burst into colour as the almond blossom takes over, so this is a particularly pleasant time to enjoy the walking here. Soon after comes the orange blossom, filling the air with a wonderful scent.

The routes included here all feel off the beaten track, and although the biggest mountain summits aren't featured, all these routes will reward you with beautiful scenery.

The footpaths are good, and it is best to always stay on them as the surrounding vegetation is usually dense and often very sharp. In the unlikely event of a rain forecast, we don't recommend walking. The paths become very slippery, with the surface becoming glutinous.

For those wanting more walking routes, Cicerone also publishes *Walking on the Costa Blanca* by Terry Fletcher. This has around 50 walks throughout the region.

Grading

Routes in this section have been assigned the following grades:

- **Easy:** Mostly on well-graded paths that are easy to follow without the need for technical navigational skills. Ascent of less than 300m.
- **Moderate:** Mostly on good paths but in more mountainous terrain and involving up to 700m of height gain. Navigation skills may be required for some sections.
- **Difficult:** High-mountain terrain with sections away from marked trails and involving up to 1100m of height gain. Navigation skills will be required for some sections.

ROUTE 44
Mallada del Llop and El Regall

Start/finish	El Castellet recreation area, Castell de Castells, ///reusing. skimpy.amid
Distance	14km
Ascent	1000m
Grade	Difficult
Time	5hr
Maps	*Costa Blanca Mountains*, Discovery Walking Guides

The Serrella mountain range, of which this route is a part, has more spectacular scenery and rock formations than any other in the region. This route enjoys some of the finest of these formations while having easy road access from the sleepy mountain village of Castell de Castells (Castle of the Castles). All these mountains are well covered in the various walking guidebooks for the region, so here we aim to offer something a little different. Prepare for 'off-path' and some rocky terrain. Although there is no proper rock scrambling involved on this route, do have your 'adventure hat' on and don't mind getting hands on rock from time to time.

We strongly recommend you only attempt this route during good, clear weather conditions, as a cloudy day would make route-finding awkward.

Access and parking

Follow CV-720 from Pedreguer to Castell de Castells. As the road passes through the village it descends to cross the river. Turn left here onto the CV-752 towards Tarbena. The El Castellet/Refugio turning is reached after just a few yards. Turn right here onto a narrow lane and keep left at the only junction. A few hundred yards further you'll come to a small parking area by the recreation area and loos.

The walk

Take the **PR-CV 149** uphill, passing the **recreation area** and various buildings. This is a well-defined wide track that is intermittently surfaced. It soon leads through pine woodland and olive groves. At a left-hand bend, a painted cross indicates

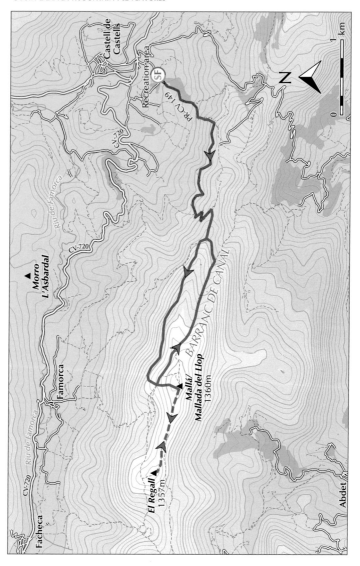

another path going straight ahead. Follow the cross on a path which levels off for a few metres before crossing a stream-bed and continuing as a smaller path that zigzags uphill through scrub and pine. After about 30 minutes you will reach a wide track. Go straight across this onto another narrow path leading into pine woods to emerge on a large track again. Turn right here, on level ground at first, and with impressive rocky outcrops to the left.

The track soon ascends quite steeply to pass a minor peak before more level ground is reached. The Barranc de Canal and Mallada del Llop now fill the view ahead.

At a high point by some old fencing/animal enclosures is a sign for Confrides/Castell de Castells. Turn towards Confrides initially, then forge a route towards the rocky peaks straight ahead.

At a col the path turns left; ignore this and go straight on.

You are now off-path on rocky terrain with an abundance of low-level scrub vegetation. Pick a way through the rocks keeping slightly right of any high points.

A few cairns mark the way now and again, but the path is vague and often disappears; just keep right of the big rocky ridge, using this as a handrail.

A large grassy levelling will be reached. This is the top of the **Barranc de Canal**. Cross this to find a small path forging a rising traverse left to right. This soon deteriorates into scree, but is never unpleasant. Continue until the gradient eases then go left across the plateau to reach the summit trig point of **Mallada del Llop**.

Extension to El Regall
This may be far enough for many walkers. Others may wish to extend the route to the neighbouring summit of 'El Regall'.

Final scree slopes to the summit with the walls of Barranc de Canal behind

From the summit of Mallada del Llop, follow a good path leading slightly north of west along the beautiful ridge for 1.5km. This section offers increasingly wonderful views over to Pla de la Casa and the other Serrella peaks, as well as down to the colourful villages dotted far below.

Return

From Mallada del Llop summit retrace steps to descend to the top of the Barranc de Canal. Here, a good path descends through the *barranco* (canyon). The huge rock walls forming either side of the *barranco* form one of the highlights of this route. While descending the *barranco*, look out for remains of the *neveros* (snow/ice pits).

Just before a holm oak on the left, and where a twin pine stands ahead, bear left at the red and white markings to traverse toward a grassy/rocky hillside. Follow a small but good path uphill, which soon affords views down to the shimmering waters of Guadalest reservoir.

At a col with a cairn, turn right onto a traverse path and retrace your steps back to the old fencing. From here you can re-join the large track used on the outward journey. Stay on this to its low point, and then go left – back onto the small path you used on the outward route. Follow this back to recreation area.

🚶 ROUTE 45
Cova del Dalt and Es Crestall

Start/finish	Puerto de Sa Creueta, Castell de Castells, ///leggy.lifted. lightbulb
Distance	7km
Ascent	250m
Grade	Easy
Time	2hr 30min–3hr
Maps	*Costa Blanca Mountains*, Discovery Walking Guides

A huge cavern, a summit and a bizarrely situated mountain-top airfield, all encountered during one relatively short walk. That's some going.

Most of the route is on small paths and the section up to the airfield is indistinct. The descent is on a wide track and easy to follow. For those wanting an even shorter walk, just visiting the cavern and summit of Es Crestall is a very worthwhile outing; it would take about one hour off the overall time.

Access and parking

The CV-752 runs between the mountain villages of Tarbena and Castell de Castells. Following this from the Tarbena direction, the parking area can be found between the 5km and 6km markings. This is immediately prior to cresting the hill at Puerto de Sa Creueta. Park in lay-bys on the right (north) side taking care not to block access for the bee-keepers and farmers.

The walk

From the parking area follow a broad track heading uphill towards Es Crestall – the peak on the skyline. After only a few metres there is an *'Atención Abejas'* sign. Beware of the beehives here. We have not experienced any problems with the

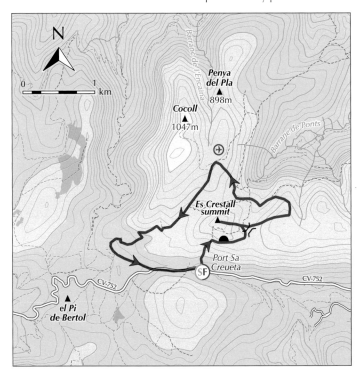

bees, but they do make their presence felt! Keeping the beehives on your left, the broad track disappears and it seems that no track continues. Have faith! Your aim is to keep on the left side of the broad gully and head towards the prominent grey and orange rocks a few hundred metres further ahead. Initially the path is vague, but keep on this trajectory and soon it becomes clearer and is marked with small cairns as it meanders up the hillside.

It is a pleasant 25 minutes of gentle uphill to reach **Cova del Dalt**. While the rest of the walk offers some splendid mountain panoramas, this is without doubt the star attraction.

Cova del Dalt has served as a shelter for people and is still used by wild animals, offering complete protection from the elements yet still providing plenty of natural light. The rock formations are beautiful and inspiring, bordering on the mind-boggling! Local archaeological societies have taken interest in the cave, as have rock climbers (evident from the shiny bolts leading up to the impressive roofs). There is a smaller chamber to the right of the main chamber, this is accessed through the same way entrance, but you will need a torch to fully appreciate the surroundings.

Exit the cave and turn left to pass by a few trees and over limestone pavement. Within a few metres go left again and follow a vague path as it climbs up a slight depression. This leads to the summit of **Es Crestall** in just a few minutes. From the summit you can enjoy views of Montgo, Caval Verd, Segaria, Benicadell, Mallarda del Llop and more.

Es Crestall summit

Retrace your steps along the path. From the small **col**, go right and walk just below the crest on its left side, heading in a generally easterly direction. A vague path comes and goes, but is not overly helpful, so pick your own way. As the rocky crest peters out a corral (ruin) can be seen ahead at a clearing. Well before reaching the corral, look out for a small cairn. Turn left here, going quite steeply down the slope towards a wooded area. A small path leads into and through the trees to emerge at a large clearing on a col, where there are several bathtubs with drinking water for livestock. A few large flat slabs are conveniently positioned as seats and offer great views over to Montgo.

Next to the slabs the land rises again and becomes filled with scrub once more. Keep left of a small ruin as you follow a faint path leading to rocks. The path turns left here, but it soon goes back right, generally heading north at first then northwest. (There are actually a few paths all leading to the same place.) A few minutes of gentle uphill leads to a surprising sight below your feet – a runway. An **Aerodrom Serveis Forestals** has been strategically positioned so that aircraft can help with control of forest fires. Thankfully the runway doesn't see too much action – so you can expect the peacefulness of the walk to continue. Cross the runway to locate a broad track. Turn left onto this track and follow it downhill to reach Corrals d'Aialt, where you will find a few buildings, and some in ruins. Once beyond the buildings go left onto the PR-CV 46 – a broad dirt track leading through almond groves. The open views ahead to Aixorta are splendid from here. It is worth considering the short walk to 'Les Arcs' while you're in the area. The starting point for that walk is at the large signboard on the main road by the 7km marker. A map shows the way. To finish, the track soon joins the **CV-752**. Go left here to return to the parking area.

ROUTE 46
Xanchet circuit

Start/finish	Viewpoint at top of Vall de Gulabdar, Polop, ///seeking. imitated.preventable
Distance	14km
Ascent	600m
Grade	Moderate
Time	4hr 30min
Maps	*Serra d'Aitana. Marina Baixa*, Editorial Piolet; *Costa Blanca Mountains*, Discovery Walking Guides

While this route may not visit any summits, it has all the hallmarks of a proper mountain day, with lots of high and impressive terrain. The tracks are good throughout, with a mix of single-track and wider trails.

Access and parking

From the N-332/A-7 coast roads, drive towards the small town of Polop. Coming from the north, this is the CV-715. Upon entering the town, turn right at the roundabout onto a road signed for Guadalest. Follow this to another roundabout and go straight across, onto a narrow but surfaced lane. Soon the tarmac runs out, but only for a short way. At a T-junction turn right and go uphill and onto a concrete road. Follow this as it rises steeply, passing beneath large crags, to arrive at a level area with benches. Park here.

The walk

The parking area marks the end of the surfaced lane, continue on foot along the unsurfaced lane that runs above a deep *barranco* (canyon) to its left. Large rock walls soon tower on either side of the track. A series of bends culminate at the **Casa de Deu** – a blue painted building. From here, take the **PR-CV 17** towards

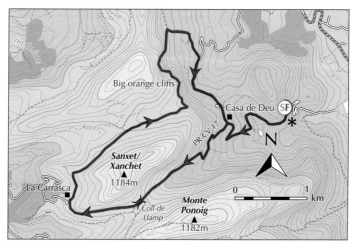

Dramatic cliffs below the Xanchet plateau

the **Coll del Llamp**. The wide track continues for much of the way to the col but becomes single track before reaching it.

Continue over the col, keeping a rocky outcrop to your left, and at a level section take the right-hand fork in the path – this is marked by a cairn. This path leads into pine woodland and begins to traverse around the base of **Xanchet** (Sanxet). Once clear of the woodland, aim for the base of a broad, rocky ridge. From here, there are fine views to the rocky serrations of Castellets ridge. A short section of fixed rope eases progress across a rocky slab, then continue traversing rightwards around the base of rocky ground to reach **La Carrasca** – a large house at a col. From here take the lower path which passes close to the house and in the direction of a prominent notch on the rock ridge ahead. Pass the base of the ridge and keep with the good path to reach a col at a large level area with a grand house on the left.

Go sharp right here onto a narrow but good path that offers wonderful views to the ridges of Bernia and Ferrer. Soon the path heads into pine woodland as it clings to the right-hand side of the *barranco*. Leave the woods behind and, at a rocky spur, the descent begins on a zigzag path. This leads under an impressive **orange cliff** before reaching an even more impressive cirque (deep bowl-shaped hollow), with huge cliffs all around.

As the path begins to trend away from the cliffs, look out for paint marks of various colours that indicate a small path leading off to the right. Turn onto this and follow it downhill to reach a broad track. Go left onto this, still heading downhill. On reaching a couple of gateposts and a chain barrier, bear right and go back uphill on a surfaced track. At a fork above a house go slightly rightwards and soon you'll re-join the outward route back to the parking area.

ROUTE 47

Bernia circuit and fort

Start/finish	Parking area at Casas de Bernia at the end of the CV-749, ///persuade.piazzas.doves
Distance	9.5km
Ascent	350m
Grade	Moderate
Time	4hr
Maps	*Serra de Bèrnia. Marina Alta*, Editorial Piolet; *Costa Blanca Mountains*, Discovery Walking Guides

Some people will only want to traverse the rocky crest of Sierra de Bernia, while to others this idea would seem preposterous. In fact, both make for wonderful mountain experiences in their own right. The path on the north side of the ridge is easy to follow and offers shade for most of the morning. Once through the *forat* (natural hole in the rock) the path is slightly less distinct. It's a good idea to plan rest stops at the *forat* and the fort as they both deserve some time for exploring and marvelling at. As with many routes in the region, this one enjoys both coastal and mountain scenery in abundance. The south side of the mountain provides no shelter from the sun.

Access and parking

From the N-332 coast road, turn onto the CV-749 and follow this through the hamlet of Pinós. Continue on this road to the high point, near the campsite (*zona acampada*). Turn left here onto the minor road leading to the Bernia restaurant, and the parking area just beyond. A large information board shows a map and various paths in the area.

The walk

From the parking area, follow a surfaced lane as it heads seawards, with the magnificent Bernia ridge to the right, dominating the landscape. The ridge can be used as a handrail for most of the route.

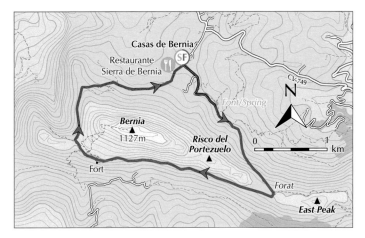

After about 15 minutes you'll reach the **font** (spring); this is also the end of the surfaced track. It's not uncommon to see people filling up with water from the *font*, although it does clearly state '*No potable*' – 'Not for drinking'!

Fingerposts, here at the *font*, show the way ahead. Follow signs for the *forat*. Taking the route in this direction gives you maximum shade for the ascent – well worth having on a warm day.

The path becomes narrow but is always easy to follow as it gently ascends the northern slopes.

Occasionally small paths deviate away from the main trail – ignore these. With the huge ridge getting ever closer, soon a short section of mild scrambling is required to negotiate a rock step. This adds fun and interest and most walkers will tackle these sections with ease. Beyond the first rocky section, the path clings to the foot of the ridge, but it soon returns to a more regular path as it passes some ancient animal enclosures.

The **forat** is a tunnel stretching all the way through the base of the mountain. Daylight penetrates, so there's no need for a torch, although it can briefly feel a little like caving.

If it's chilly on the northern side of the ridge, make swift progress through the *forat* (on hands and knees for most) to the sunny southern side where it is sure to be much warmer. Views from the southern side are a contrast to the north, with wide open vistas to the Mediterranean.

Navigation is straightforward on the south side too. Keep the big ridge to your right and follow well-maintained paths that for the most part follow a traverse

The south side of the forat

line. After a few minutes there is an option to divert to the cave paintings of Ermita del Vicari, although there's not much to see.

The main track soon descends by some gigantic boulders. This is a nice resting place and provides small pockets of shade. Historically these boulders provided much-needed shelter for animals during the intense heat of summer.

Large expanses of scree lie ahead, but thankfully the path carves out an easy route through, soon passing the welcome shade of a large holm oak. Beyond here, there are some sections of mild scrambling, but mostly the path has been improved so much there is little call to use your hands. It's well worth pausing to turn around and marvel at the **Bernia ridge** – this is arguably the best place to view it.

Turning to look towards the onward route, you'll have a clear view of the mountains of Puig Campana, Ponoch, Aitana and Xanchet.

Continuing on the route, you will soon reach the **fort**, which is worth exploring. Then find a perch on the ancient ramparts and soak up the tremendous view.

The path now continues beyond the fort. Follow this, heading generally northwest at first and following signs for Casas de Bernia. The path will trend to the right below the western nose of the Bernia ridge, and then it will lead back to the north side; there are captivating views of the rocky Peña Severino ridge on the left. The path turns right again and widens as the descent back to **Casas de Bernia** begins.

The **restaurant** next to the parking area offers freshly cooked local cuisine in a rustic setting. A small patio area by the entrance gives panoramic views along the Bernia ridge. Note: the restaurant can often appear to be closed – give the door a good push to check, as it probably is open!

TRAIL RUNNING

Enjoying winter running high up on Raco Roig (Route 51)

🏃 TRAIL RUNNING

Setting out on Route 49 with Aixorta looming in the distance

Here we offer a mix of mountain circuits, summits and coastal routes. They are all on good tracks that will be a mix of single-track technical and broad unsurfaced road type trails. The routes have been chosen for their diversity and quality. Mountain running is popular in this region, with very well-organised races most weeks. This means trails are usually kept in good condition, with spiky vegetation regularly pruned. Beware though, that wearing shorts will lead to scratched legs if venturing off-path.

It will always be a little cooler in the mountains, so choose to run high-up on the warmer days and aim for the coast on the cooler days. If temperatures are particularly high during your stay, an early start may be needed for the longer routes.

Unlike running in the UK, it is rare to find water in the mountains, so it is vital to be self-sufficient and carry plenty.

Grading
Routes in this section have been assigned the following grades:

- **Moderate:** Mostly on good paths but in more mountainous terrain and involving up to 700m of height gain. Expect steep ascents/descents. Navigation skills may be required for some sections.

- **Difficult:** High-mountain terrain with sections away from marked trails and involving up to 1100m of height gain. Long sections of steep ascent/descent. Navigation skills will be required for some sections.

ROUTE 48
Castell d'Axia

Start/finish	Llosa de Camacho, ///redid.best.familiarity
Distance	14km
Ascent	650m
Grade	Moderate
Time	2–3hr
Maps	*El Montgó. Parc Natural*, Editorial Piolet; *Serra de Bèrnia. Marina Alta*, Editorial Piolet

Driving along the CV-720 from Pedreguer to Alcalalí, it would be so easy to dismiss these mountains as unremarkable. Yet they have much to offer anyone who comes to discover the beauty of the 'Castle of the Princess'. A mix of wide tracks on the lower slopes and fabulous single track higher up, and all well maintained, make the route straightforward to follow. The cleared summit area, complete with ruined castle, is a highlight; and from here the view to the orange Montgo cliffs dominates. The strata of limestone hints to a tormented past, with huge rock waves in the landscape. The terrain underfoot makes for enjoyable running the whole way.

Access and parking

From the N-332 at Pedreguer turn onto the CV-720 and follow this towards Alcalalí. Llosa de Camacho is approximately 4km along this road. There is ample parking near the pharmacy which is at the top end of the village and signposted.

The run

From the pharmacy, run back to the main road and go uphill for a short way to a left turn. Take this good track – leading downhill at first but soon turning into a steep ascent. After a series of hairpin bends, find the unsurfaced track that leads off rightwards. This is the **PR-CV 53**. Now follow this as it ascends more gently, passing the occasional *finca*. At the **Font de la Tia Xima**, and signposted, is your

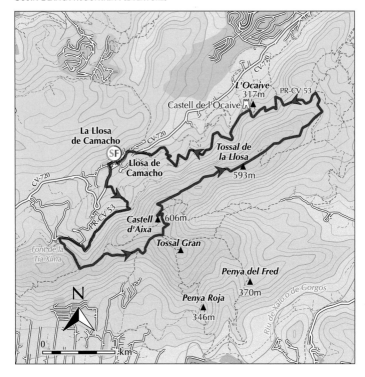

route to 'Castell d'Axia'. Turn sharply left to go steeply uphill, soon to pass a quaint house on the right. The track deteriorates a little, and narrows in places, as it leads up to a col, from where you can enjoy impressive views into the Jalón valley.

Go left here on an initially faint path. Stick with it – it gets better.

Lots of gentle ascent lies ahead and ever more delightful views towards the coast. Ignore the small path that turns off left and goes more steeply toward the summit, and instead stay with the yellow and white 'PR' waymarkers. These lead to a wooded area and a ruined corral/farm-building. (And note: there are footpaths leading down towards Jalón – ignore these.) Shortly before you reach the building the path becomes indistinct and branches out in different directions; keep aiming for the building. With yet more wonderful views over the Jalón valley and to El Peñón de Ifach on the coast, this is a good place for a breather.

Continue on a good path to reach another col, and from here take the left fork. Initially this is fairly level terrain, but it soon steepens as the summit nears. Terracing of the land is more obvious now. Follow the path as it weaves through the abandoned terraces and up to the summit and the **Castell d'Aixa** (Castle of the Princess of Aixa). Almost nothing remains of the castle, but don't be put off – from this summit the vistas are among the finest in the region: the jagged outline of Segaria to the north, Montgo to the east, and the Bernia ridge to the south. Welcome to ridge country!

From the summit follow waymarkers and cairns, first in a northerly, then a northeasterly direction, on an excellent high-level path, and aiming towards the sea. There are a couple of path junctions – just keep following the yellow and white paint and signs that eventually point southwestwards towards Castell de l'Ocaive. At a final col there is the option to make a short detour to visit **Castell de l'Ocaive** or continue down on the **PR-CV 53**. The castle (recently rebuilt) is only a few minutes detour and worth it. And beware! This castle is built very close to the top of a huge cliff, so take care!

The waymarked PR route now descends below these cliffs, and soon you find yourself directly underneath a huge and impressive overhanging orange wall with a small cave at its base. The cave is also worth a scrambly detour.

At the signpost below the cliff follow the PR route towards Font de l'Ocaive. The route has good waymarking; take care to stick to the route as there are numerous other paths leading off into the surrounding farmland. Soon the path passes below a small building, and then takes a left turn to go directly through the front garden of a small house! Immediately after passing through the garden, you find

Winter running on Castell d'Axia

the Font de L'Ocaive complete with information board for those wanting some historical and cultural input.

Uphill again on a good track towards a fairytale house on the hillside. Stay below this, and start to keep a keen look-out for the yellow and white paint as the path will soon become vague for a while. Then after a short uphill section through almond and olive groves, your rocky path turns right onto a wide track, and soon comes to a chain barrier. Beyond this, lie a few minutes of contouring through the tended farmland to where another track merges from the left. Ignore this point's PR paint and instead continue on the surfaced track as it descends back to **Llosa de Camacho**.

After a good few hours in the mountains, a treat is surely in store. The friendly Emilio's Bar in the centre of Llosa serves food and drink.

 # ROUTE 49

Aixorta and Les Arcs

Start/finish	Les Arcs parking area, CV-752, Castell de Castells, /// homages.heaps.fondly
Distance	15km
Ascent	625m
Grade	Difficult
Time	2hr
Maps	*Serra d'Aitana. Marina Baixa*, Editorial Piolet; *Costa Blanca Mountains*, Discovery Walking Guides

This route visits the Penya Alta summit of Aixorta at 1219m. Much of the route lies on the northern slopes of the mountain, thus offering shade and making it a good choice on warmer days.

Lots of wide, runnable tracks in a remote setting, yet having conveniently easy access. There is plenty of single-track running along the route too, and this is enjoyed in outstanding scenery, with some of the finest views Costa Blanca has to offer. Navigation is mostly straightforward, but particular care should be taken on higher ground with smaller paths. A long, sweeping descent from Font de Teixos includes compressed gravel, soil and concrete terrains.

Access and parking

Approach can be from either Tarbena or Castell de Castells. From the N-332 coast road, turn onto the CV-755 at Altea and follow this to Callosa d'en Sarrià. Once in this small town, turn onto the CV-715 and follow signs for the Fonts del Algar. Carry on past these, and on through the pretty village of Bolulla. The road now becomes a mountain switchback, and a mecca for cyclists. As the road levels out, stay on the main road and pass through the mountain village of Tarbena. Just beyond the village you'll reach a crest and turn left at the sign for the CV-752 to Castell de Castells. Follow this to the 7km road mark and turn left by a large information board. Follow the unsurfaced road for a few hundred metres to reach a large solitary house. Park considerately at a clearing on the right.

The run

Follow the surfaced lane (PR-CV 151) gently downhill through almond groves below, but not yet close to, the impressive north face of Penya Alta d'Aixorta.

Turn right following a fingerpost for Les Arcs (1.8km further on), then soon bear right at another sign for Les Arcs. The wide track now begins to ascend. At a junction, turn off right towards Penya Escoda and Les Arcs, (left is for Font de Teixos), and follow the wide, level track to pass a casita (cottage). Turn left here,

Les Arcs

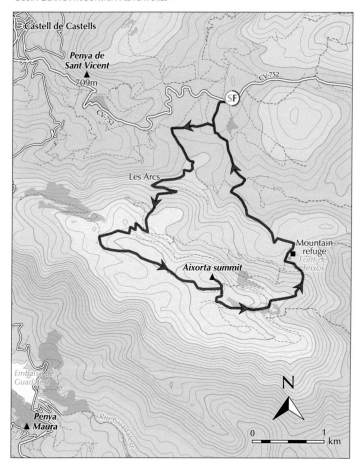

again keeping to the Les Arcs route, and stick with the yellow/white occasional markings on the path. Views to Mallada del Llop soon open up and the route becomes single track as it gently rises towards craggy ground. At a fork, go left and follow rocky steps to the wonderful sight that is **Les Arcs**.

About 30m back from the arches is a small path leading steeply uphill. Follow this to a junction and go left here onto more level terrain to reach the wide, unsurfaced track after about four minutes. Go slightly right and uphill on this track through pine woodland. At a sharp bend, a sign indicates 'Font dels Teixos 4.6km'. Turn left here onto a rough gravel track leading steeply uphill and through pine woodland until you get to a crest at a clearing. Go right on a tiny track for a short way until you reach the big track once more. Now go left on the main track as it wiggles uphill – revealing ever more impressive views, that even include Ibiza on a really clear day.

Turn right at a sharp bend and 'Deposito Contra Incendios' sign. This leads slightly downhill to a *casita*. But a few metres short of the house, turn left, pass through a chained entrance and immediately take the uphill fork in the path. There are more splendid views of Mallada del Llop and Aitana from here.

The next few kilometres are delightful single-track mountain terrain with all the joy that brings. Pass a ruin at a level section of path and continue towards light woodland and small rock towers on the left. After a few hundred metres, pass another larger ruin, where a couple of vague paths split off; stick to the clearest path.

Just prior to reaching another ruin by the edge of a sizeable and partly cultivated clearing, take the left fork onto a vague path heading towards a jumble of boulders to the right of a rocky crest. Contour along this path, keeping the clearing to your right, and you'll soon reach a better path. Go left onto this, ascending to reach a lone pine by a col with rock spires. Go left again, climbing towards clumps of holm oak, to reach the summit via scree paths. Yellow and white PR markers help show the way.

The **Aixorta summit** panorama includes: Segaria, Montgo, Sierra de Bernia, Puig Campana, Ponoch, Sierra de Aitana, Serrella and Mallada del Llop, to name a few. The small village nestling below Aitana is the tourist hotspot of Guadalest.

Retrace your steps to the col with the lone pine and descend left here on a good path leading into pine woodland. While descending, note the striking and shapely peak to the right; this is the main summit of Sierra de Bernia. Drop down through woodland to reach the 'Hansel and Gretel'-style **mountain refuge**. Join the wide track here and follow it downhill, keeping left after 50m, where signed for Guadalest.

After a few hundred metres, ignore a track that goes sharp right, and stay on the main track leading under the huge crags of Aixorta. Once well clear of these crags, the track goes over a crest, and shortly afterwards reaches a junction. Turn right here to regain the outbound route.

From here on, stay on the wide track (it is easiest underfoot and most likely welcome after this big route). So, unless you want to revisit Les Arcs, don't deviate from the wide and mostly surfaced track to reach the parking area.

ROUTE 50
Corral de la Llacuna

Start/finish	Large surfaced lay-by on the CV-720 Benigembla to Castell de Castells road, ///class.paradox.antonym
Distance	12km
Ascent	500m
Grade	Moderate
Time	1hr 30min
Maps	*Costa Blanca Mountains*, Discovery Walking Guides

With wide tracks for most of the way, this is a relatively easy-going route through backcountry that provides a wilderness feeling from the off. The landscape is dramatic and untamed, with a peaceful run being assured, and the soundtrack of abundant wildlife for company.

The well-tended area of Corral de la Llacuna seems quite peculiar due to its remote setting. Roughly translated this means – 'small farm building suitable as an animal dwelling and set by a shallow lagoon'. Stand awhile and picture the scene, it all fits perfectly.

Access and parking
From the N-332 turn onto the CV-750 just south of Benissa and follow signs for Jalón/Xaló. Go through this small town, staying on the CV-750 in the direction of Alcalalí. At a T-junction on the outskirts of Alcalalí turn left onto the CV-720 towards Parcent. Soon you'll come to signs for Castell de Castells; follow these, staying on the CV-720. After Benigembla there is a large lay-by on the left, soon after the 30km marker and immediately after crossing the river. Park here.

The run
From the parking area, follow the wide forestry track as it meanders in a generally southerly direction, while ascending steadily. After a few minutes a minor track descends toward the bottom of the valley bottom; ignore this, and keep going

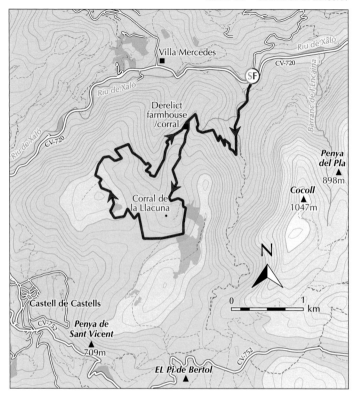

uphill. After about 15 minutes there are tended beehives (*abejas*) on the right and a **derelict farmhouse** to the left. The terrain levels out and the view now opens up. A blob of blue/green paint and a small cairn heading off left into the scrub shows the onward route as it now becomes technical single track.

From here on, pay close attention to the route, as the path is narrow and indistinct. Small cairns help mark the way through the scrub vegetation. After a few minutes of sustained uphill progress, the terrain eases once more and you'll reach a wider track. This bears leftwards to skirt the large hollow ahead – the well-tended **Corral de la Llacuna**. Seemingly miles from anywhere and extraordinarily peaceful, it is an oasis-like experience. Take a moment to imagine the shallow lagoon that may once have filled the hollow below.

Horses getting saddled up at the derelict farmhouse

The route soon heads uphill again, only more gently now. Take time to enjoy views towards the slender and rocky Caballo Verd ridge, and to look back at Sierra d'Alfaro. Closer by, look out for sparrowhawks, wall lizards, butterflies and many varieties of wildflowers. Keep quiet, tread softly and the ibex may pose too!

Just a few minutes more gives increasingly wonderful views over to the mountains of Serrella, Aixorta, Mallarda de Llop and Aitana.

Shortly after the corral, pass a more modern building before beginning another uphill section along the wide and occasionally newly surfaced track. Light pine woodland will occasionally provide shade or shelter from the wind, and by now some shade may be appreciated.

The return route stays on this wide track the whole way. During 2019 some of this track was given a concrete surface – which is a shame, but it does mean there's a more solid surface for the fast descent. For those not keen to be on such a hard surface, there is regular respite, and the margins of the concrete are often runnable.

The quaint and traditional mountain village of Castell de Castells has cafés and restaurants serving good-quality local cuisine. Castell d'Inés is particularly worthy of note – they can whip up a culinary masterpiece for the most discerning of palettes.

ROUTE 51

Les Arcs and Raco Roig

Start/finish	Les Arcs parking area, CV-752, Castell de Castells, /// homages.heaps.fondly
Distance	11km
Ascent	350m
Grade	Moderate
Time	1hr 20min
Maps	*Serra de Bèrnia. Marina Alta*, Editorial Piolet; *Costa Blanca Mountains*, Discovery Walking Guides

This route is a blend of broad trails and technical single track through truly uplifting scenery. Views of the vast Bolulla canyon is a highlight of the outward run, and the mighty summit of Aixorta captivates attention for the return leg.

Access and parking

Approach can be from either Tarbena or Castell de Castells. From the N-332 coast road, turn onto the CV-755 at Altea, and follow this to Callosa d'en Sarrià. Once in this small town, turn onto the CV-715 and follow signs for the Fonts del Alga. Go past these, and through the pretty village of Bolulla, to find the road is now a mountain switchback, and a Mecca for cyclists. It levels out as you pass through the mountain village of Tarbena. Just beyond the village, and on reaching a crest, turn left at the sign for Castell de Castells, on the CV-752. Follow this to the 7km road marker and turn left by a large information board. Follow the unsurfaced road for a few hundred metres to reach a large solitary house. Park considerately at a clearing on the right.

The run

From the parking area, continue along the unpaved track as it bends to the left and gently descends, passing an old *finca* on the right. During springtime the cherry and almond trees will be in bloom in the surrounding fields.

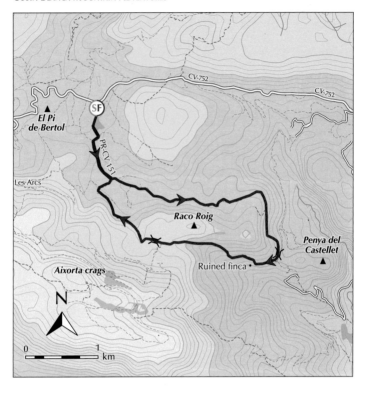

At a junction follow signs left for Aljub Xorquet, **PR-CV151**, and stick with this initially broad track for a few hundred more metres. It then becomes single track as it forges a way through the almond terraces and into light woodland. Soon the vegetation becomes low scrub and views open up. Looking back, the big ridge is Mallarda del Llop and Barranc del Canal; looking forward is the magnificent chasm of Bolulla canyon, with the Bernia ridge standing proud in the distance. The terrain is fairly level and is ideal for running. And it stays like this all the way to the **col** below Penya del Castellet. Here, at a junction with a surfaced lane, turn right and go downhill for about 20m, until you come to a footpath on the right; follow this towards a ruined **finca**.

In the distance is the **col** this route is aiming for, and it's all single track and gently uphill to get there. Passing by more ruined buildings, the path remains

Perfect single-track running on the Raco Roig trails

good and easy to follow. Views of the huge Aixorta crags dominate beyond the col.

Once at the col, go straight ahead at a cairned junction, then on into pine woodland. Care is needed here to stick with the path as it becomes vague.

Soon the descent begins and, leaving the woodland behind, you are now on the left of a ravine. Look up rightwards to see the impressive 'window' in the limestone crags. There is a rocky section for about 100m before the trail reverts to less technical running, and then the track widens again. At a signposted junction turn right and follow this wide track back to the outward route.

✸ ROUTE 52
Castell de Granadella

Start/finish	Hípica riding school, Cumbre del Sol, Benitachell, /// glacier.movers.estate
Distance	7.5km
Ascent	300m
Grade	Moderate
Time	1hr 20min
Maps	None available

Coastal running on good and often rocky tracks leading to a castle on a peninsula. This route offers a great vantage point over coves and rocky cliffs. Below is the gorgeous beach of Granadella – a perfect swimming spot. The route has a fairly long steep section towards the end, so it's worth holding back some energy for it.

Cumbre del Sol is a modern development of upmarket villas and apartments, most of which overlook the Mediterranean. Immediately north of this development lies the Granadella nature reserve, which, thank goodness, is protected from further housing development. But what it isn't protected from is fire! In 2016 a forest fire raged through the area, burning everything in its path. Yet by 2018 the landscape had already made a dramatic recovery and is now lush with flora and fauna. It's still missing the pine trees, but they'll be back.

Access and parking

From the N-332 just north of Benissa, turn onto the CV-740 towards Teulada, and continue to Benitatxell. Go straight over the crossroads in the centre of town and, at the next set of traffic lights, take the right fork towards Cumbre del Sol and Platjes/Playas. After a few hundred metres of ascent you'll reach a fine viewpoint. Then carry on and descend, passing a large school on the right, into the *urbanización*. Go slight left at the second turning, following signs for Centro Hípico and follow these to Plaza Cumbre del Sol/Girasoles. Park opposite the riding school.

The run

From the **Centro Hípico** (riding school), follow the wide track heading northeast into the **Granadella nature reserve**. To the left is a wide ravine, and this forms part of the return route. After a few minutes, a large information board displays various route options, and shows the wildlife and history of the area. Follow signs for Castell de Granadella, leading through a chained-off section of track and out towards the sea. At each junction, follow the PR-CV 354 – an excellent track making for enjoyable running. The end of the 'easier' running comes when the track begins to descend more abruptly and cliffs can be seen nearby. What lies ahead is beautiful single-track rocky terrain, with the path perched high above the turquoise waters far below. On a clear day, look straight ahead (north) for surprise views of Ibiza.

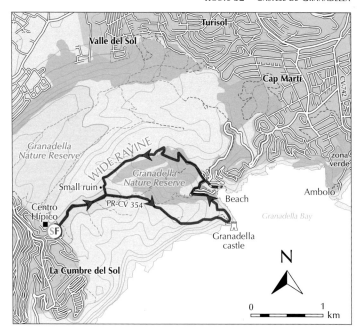

Care is required on the descent to the **castle** – the limestone is sharp, uneven and unforgiving. The vegetation bites too. Take a moment to admire the almost 300-year-old castle and its 3m-thick walls.

Retrace your steps for a few metres from the castle and continue towards Granadella bay. This gives the first proper ascent of the run and, although short, it is over technical and exposed terrain.

A short descent into the mouth of a *barranco* (canyon) precedes a longer uphill section with increasingly impressive views over **Granadella bay**. The track improves and becomes a surfaced lane servicing a few rather fine villas perched on the hillside. A steep descent leads to the **Granadella beach**. In high season and at weekends the restaurant will be open.

Retrace your steps from the beach towards the road and at a junction go straight ahead at the signpost for the PR-CV 354, on an initially surfaced track. At another junction, take the left-hand fork along the rocky bed of the ravine. This makes for fun running. After just a few more metres take a path going off left up a series of steep steps climbing out of the ravine. Finally levelling out at a

235

Granadella beach far below the trail can be visited during the run

small ruin, keep following orange dots and yellow/white markers to reach the wide track of the outward route. Follow this back to the road.

 ROUTE 53
Sierra de Olta

Start/finish	Zona d'Acampada, Olta/Calpe, ///counteract.driving. shrouds
Distance	12km
Ascent	450m
Grade	Moderate
Time	1hr 45min
Map	None available

This route offers a coastal feel while navigating up and around Olta, on the outskirts of the bustling resort of Calpe (Calp). A variety of wide tracks and technical single track, with sections of limestone pavement on the summit plateau, all go towards making this a fantastically diverse run. Scenery is of coast and mountain, including wonderful panoramas of the nearby Bernia ridge.

It's worth noting that the bulk of the ascent follows a rocky gully with easy scrambling. It is not uncommon to come across mountain goats on the Olta plateau. Tread lightly for these chance encounters.It's worth noting that the bulk of the ascent follows a rocky gully with easy scrambling. It is not uncommon to come across mountain goats on the Olta plateau. Tread lightly for these chance encounters.

Access and parking

From the N-332 turn off at the Calpe Sur exit and follow signs for the train station (Estación). Pass the station and go over the level crossing. As the road wind its way uphill, follow signs for the 'Zona d'Acampada' (campsite). Park in either of the two small car parks next to the campsite.

The run

A marked trail leaves the car park and runs alongside the **campsite**, this is the **PR-CV 340**. Follow this until you reach the large signboard showing maps of the

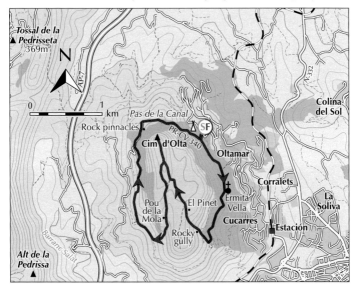

The summit of Olta offers wonderful views of the serrated Bernia ridge

mountain and the various hiking routes. Stay on the PR-CV 340 following the route to 'Ermita Vella'. This is a wide track with a gentle incline, and there are a couple of water stations along the way if needed.

Ermita Vella has picnic tables and shade as well as public loos. Keep on the main track as it steadily rises uphill; high up on the right and just right of a broad and **rocky gully**, is a prominent pine tree. The gully provides the meat of the ascent. At its base is a sign for 'Cim d'Olta'; strike up into the gully here. The path becomes narrow and rocky, and some may choose to use hands on occasion.

Emerging at the top of the gully, another signpost directs the way to 'Cim d'Olta'. But some people may wish to take a short diversion to the prominent tree **'El Pinet'**, with its welcome shade and fine views over the coast.

Limestone pavement leads to a saddle where a ruin 'El Corralet' nestles. Turn right at the ruin to reach a col between rocky outcrops. Turn right again at the col, still following signs for 'Cim d'Olta' which can now be seen – marked by a large metal post. Dramatic views over to the sinuous Bernia ridge can now be fully enjoyed.

Although not a high mountain, the **summit of Olta** (587m) is very exposed, so it's worth having an extra layer of clothing and not hanging around too long.

Retrace your steps back to the col and turn right here, still on the PR-CV 340, and follow this track towards Pou de la Mola. This is an excellent single-track descent, but beware of the limestone outcrops underfoot. The path levels out as terraces take over the landscape. Turn left here, and after a few metres you will arrive back at 'El Corralet'. And now turn right here and follow more delightful trails toward **Pou de la Mola**. The path gently descends into a broad, pine-filled gully, with towering cliffs on the left, and views out to sea straight ahead. When you reach a sign for 'Circuit Principal', bear rightwards, and head back to the forestry track. This good track is followed for much of the return route and provides some wonderful views to the mountains, particularly Sierra de Bernia. Keep with the PR-CV 340 the whole time – the route is marked out in yellow and white at various points along the way. Just before a steep section comes 'Finca Pastor' – complete with makeshift benches, it's not a bad place to stop for a rest.

Continue steeply. Although this section is quite short-lived, you'll need to keep some energy in reserve. Big rock walls lie above. And to the right, the **huge pinnacle** surely deserves an ascent, too! Immediately after this comes a short descent and re-ascent to **'Pas de la Canal'**. Note how the rock faces here change from orange to white, marking the change from south-facing to north-facing.

The broad track ends here and a delightful single-track descent through pine woodland leads back to the **camping area** and finish line.

⭐ ROUTE 54

Puig Campana

Start/finish	Parking beside bridge beyond Font de Molí, Finestrat, /// rums.sums.skydiver
Distance	15.5km
Ascent	1070m
Grade	Difficult
Time	3hr
Maps	*Serra d'Aitana. Marina Baixa*, Editorial Piolet; *Costa Blanca Mountains*, Discovery Walking Guides

Not only is this the most iconic mountain in the region, it also offers the finest trail and mountain running on top-notch trails that are mostly well signposted. The level of ascent and descent make this route feel tough, but there is plenty of gentle terrain in-between, meaning it will be runnable for many, apart from the steep, rocky section between Col de Pouet and the summit, which will more likely be walking territory.

Another appealing factor is that around half of the route will be in the shade, bringing better temperatures for running.

Access and parking

Follow the CV-767 to Finestrat and, once in the village, turn onto a narrow lane at the sign for Font de Molí. This ascends steeply to the font. The water from the font is good and popular with the locals, so don't forget to fill your bottles. There are various lay-bys shortly after passing the Font de Molí. Park in any of these; or if full, park at the font.

The run

Cross the bridge and gain a wide track, aiming for the mountain. Go left at a sign for Col de Pouet 4.4km on the PR-CV 13 289.

Remain on the excellent wide track as it steadily ascends under the south and then west faces. This part of the mountain is mesmerising, with hundreds of metres of vertical rock, and spires and pinnacles a-plenty.

As the trail undulates in a northeasterly direction, and after about 4.5km, you will reach the **Refugio José Manuel Vera Catral**. This refuge is a metal shack in the woods, located directly on the trail. Basic as it is, should the weather take a turn for the worse, this would come as a welcome sight. The path passes to the right of the *refugio* before heading uphill once more to gain the **Col de Pouet** in a few hundred metres.

If very steep ascents and descents aren't your thing, this section up to the summit can be missed out. But for the full 'Puig' effect it is time to get a sweat on!

From the Col de Pouet follow signs for 'Cumbre/Cim'. These lead slightly rightwards and always uphill, with navigation well marked and straightforward. Soon the path becomes narrow single track, through woodland at first, and then rock and scree. Yellow and white paint markings show the best route for the next 2km, until you reach a broad col. At this point, **Pic Prim** is to your right, and a huge gully lies below and straight ahead. The highest point of **Puig Campana** is to your left. Follow the sign, and more yellow and white paint on occasionally vague paths as they lead around to the south side of the summit, traversing more easily, before a final dog-leg bend leads to the top.

Views from the summit of Puig Campana are stupendous, so it is most definitely worth taking a breather to soak up the atmosphere. Roldan's Notch can be seen over on the south summit and slightly further afield lie the Divino, Sella, Castellets ridge, Aitana, Bernia ridge, El Peñón de Ifach, and Montgo, to name a few. When the air is clear, Ibiza may be seen too, rising out of the sea slightly to the right of Montgo.

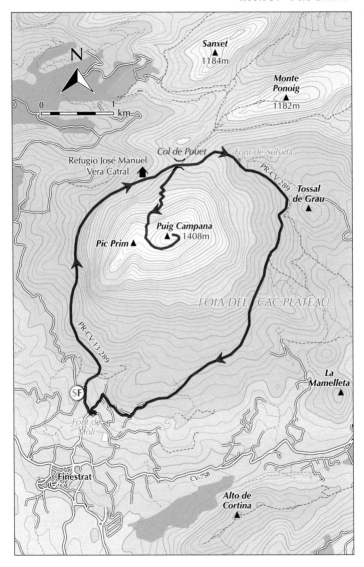

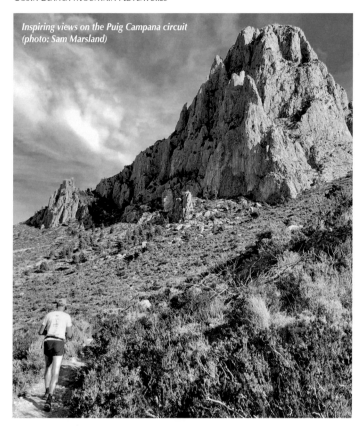

Inspiring views on the Puig Campana circuit (photo: Sam Marsland)

Retrace your steps for the 2km back to the main path **PR-CV 289** and turn right onto this. The steep descent from the summit requires care but is mostly runnable, and fun. About 400m after reaching the main path, you'll come to the small green oasis of **Font de Solsida**. There's no drinking water here, but you can enjoy a refreshing splash.

Continue on wonderful trails through woodland and scrub. Again, this is all runnable with care. A broad gully can be seen to the right, and the path becomes vague as it descends to cross this, with only occasional cairns to mark the way through the low-level scrub. You are now crossing the Foia del Cac plateau.

Some 700m after crossing another broad gully below Els Amanellos, pass ruins of a cave-house on the right. A further 150m will take you to a crossroads; go straight across and follow a sign for 'Font del Molí in 2.1km'.

In 1.1km, and just after passing close to a couple of large houses, you'll come to a minor road. Turn right, following the Font del Molí sign.

After 150m this road becomes an unsurfaced track. Stay on it as it loops around the broad gully, before coming to a T-junction. Go left, and almost immediately cross a bridge over an aqueduct.

You will reach the main road in 150m. Turn left to return to the parking area.

 ROUTE 55

Penya Gros and Forada

Start/finish	Alcalà de la Jovada, ///explored.peacemakers.briefed
Distance	11km
Ascent	300m
Grade	Moderate
Time	1hr 40min
Maps	*Les Valls de la Marina Alta. Parc Natural de la Marjal de Pego-Oliva*, Editorial Piolet; *Costa Blanca Mountains*, Discovery Walking Guides

Visiting the fabled 'Forada' and running on high-mountain trails that are mostly well marked is an absolute delight. Sections of the ascent require careful footwork due to loose and often sharp limestone, so it's not all plain sailing. For those comfortable in exposed places and scrambling, it is possible to traverse the top of the *forat* (natural hole in the rock) at about UK scrambling grade 3.

Access and parking

From the CV-715 Pego–Orba road, turn onto the CV712 towards Vall d'Ebo. This meanders its way into the hills, passing the hamlet of Vall d'Ebo before arriving at the small village of Alcalà de la Jovada. Parking is available near the public swimming pool on the edge of the village.

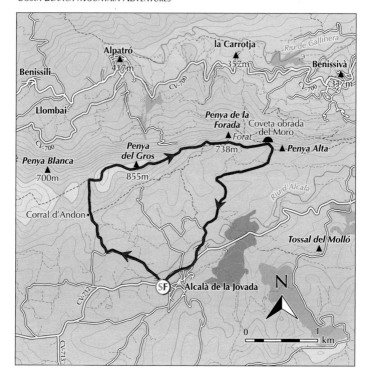

The run

Back-track to the main road and go straight over this towards the campsite, following a tarmac lane uphill. At a fallen signpost, keep to the main track, aiming in the general direction of the ridge. Turn right at the next junction.

The tarmac ends at **'Corral d'Andon'** (ruin). Turn left here onto a good track leading into a U-shaped valley with a rocky spur high above on the right. Continue along the valley bottom, passing through a cluster of almond trees to reach a col. From here, there are fine views into the Vall de Gallinera.

Turn right toward cliffs and follow the cairned path uphill. The path soon becomes rocky and slightly vague. When the terrain levels out again, bear left then right to follow the saddled ridge (cairns). Views over to Benicadell and Al Azraq Castell are outstanding from this vantage.

Enjoying wide trails and big views on the Forada descent

To reach the summit trig point, bear left as the ground starts to ascend. This leads on to **Penya del Gros** (855m) and this route's high point. From here, retrace steps a short way before continuing leftwards (east-north-east) along the ridge towards the now-visible *forat*.

The path is at times vague. Stay slightly right (south) of the crest all the way to the *forat*. It is well worth taking some time to explore the *forat*.

From the *forat*, descend to reach the large track continuing eastwards along the ridge, passing a small stone structure/ruin. Continue on this good, rocky path to reach the impressive **'Coveta obrada del Moro'** which on first glance looks like any other ruined farmhouse-type structure. But look closer, venture inside and you'll find a perfectly constructed cave built into the hillside. Talk about a room with a view! This makes for an ideal shelter on a breezy day, too.

Retrace your steps for about 200m until back on rock slabs. Turn left here at the yellow/white paint heading towards a farmhouse.

Now the route is single track for a short way, passing through an almond and fig grove, towards the farmhouse. There is a three-way split here – take the middle, wide track, which goes into a dip on the left of a rise. Then, when another wide track joins from the right, go left towards a large ruin, and bear left again in front of the ruin.

Soon after, at a fork, turn right onto a heavily rutted track and right again at an MTB/BTT sign. Soon you'll reach another wider track; go right at another MTB/BTT sign and pass through more almond groves. The track becomes surfaced; turn left at a junction to reach the road, and follow this back to **Alcalà**.

 ROUTE 56

Barranco del Infierno circuit

Start/finish	Fleix, Vall de Laguar, ///popular.wiki.waft
Distance	13km
Ascent	800m
Grade	Difficult
Time	2hr 30min
Map	*Les Valls de la Marina Alta. Parc Natural de la Marjal de Pego-Oliva*, Editorial Piolet; *Costa Blanca Mountains*, Discovery Walking Guides

Without reaching any summits, but incorporating lots of climbing, this route is hugely satisfying and enjoys a big feel. The gaping chasm of the canyon is mesmerising and adds dramatic effect. The trails are excellent throughout and the whole route is runnable (though many, no doubt, will choose to 'jog' the steeper uphills!). Waymarking is good, too, meaning runners can focus more on the running and the epic scenery. For many visitors this is the number one place for scenic beauty.

Access and parking

From the village of Orba, take the CV-718 towards Fontilles and Campell. Drive through the narrow high street of Campell and continue for three to four minutes to reach the village of Fleix. There is a large parking area opposite the school on the edge of the village.

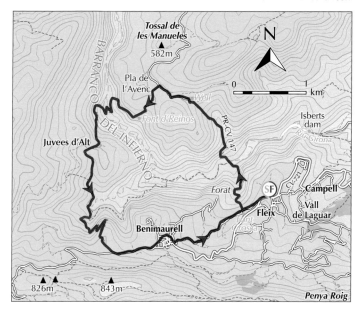

The run

Follow the Benimaurell road for about 100m, turn right at **PR-CV 147** for Juvees d'En Mig and go downhill passing the wash-house/**Font Grossa**. Shortly after this go right onto the path towards Juvees d'En Mig – still the PR-CV 147. This single track is rocky but stepped and well maintained.

Soon you arrive at the **forat** (natural hole in the rock). Go through this to reach wide open views over the dramatic valley below. Zigzag downwards, crossing a riverbed and continue all the way down to the valley bottom and a much larger riverbed. This is the exit from Barranco del Infierno. (For those wanting a longer run, it's possible to follow the riverbed downstream to Isberts dam (disused) – about 20 minutes each way.)

Go straight over the riverbed following yellow and white paint markings onto more stepped zigzags. This side of the valley is likely to be in the sun and much warmer! When the terrain begins to level out, look out for a small dwelling on the left, and straight ahead is a **well**. At the well, turn right then immediately left onto a surfaced lane, and follow this uphill. Bear right at the crest and descend, passing a partly renovated house. Then, after the next house, go left at PR-CV 147 sign for

247

Running on the ancient trails high above the Barranco del Infierno

Juvees d'Alt. This leads to the large open area of **Pla de l'Avenc**. Signs for Font d' Reinos and Barranco del Infierno are displayed here.

Follow the signs for Barranco del Infierno, passing through almond groves, before descending to **Font d'Reinos** (fresh water here). This section now gives more delightful single-track running all the way back down to the riverbed (and the entrance for **Barranco del Infierno**). Go upstream (right) following yellow and white markers for about 50m until the path bears left to begin the next ascent.

This is a long ascent on good tracks that do eventually level out – honest! At the levelling, turn right at the PR-CV 147 sign towards Benimaurell. This leads onto a wide track heading for the abandoned hamlet of **Juvees d'Alt**. Superb views can be savoured from here.

From Juvees d'Alt, go left, then immediately left again at the PR sign for Benimaurell. This follows yet more great single track, descending to pass a building and, soon afterwards, a large ruin on the side of a wide gully. Continue down, then join another *barranco* (canyon), following the path alongside it, towards the impressive and dominant cliffs high up. The route then goes up, on what is quite a long ascent, to skirt around the cliffs on the left. When the terrain levels out again, follow the path through olive and almond groves, passing a large white house on your right. Go left onto the surfaced lane towards **Benimaurell** village (900m), where you then skirt around its left edge and follow signs for Fleix.

About 30m after L'Hedrera bar, bear left and go steeply down a concrete lane, passing the font and the wash-house, and return to **Fleix** in 1.5km.

ROAD
CYCLING

Alpine conditions on the Serrella tour (Route 60)

🚴 ROAD CYCLING

Road cycling is huge in this region, with professional teams flocking here to train throughout the winter. These big teams bring investment in infrastructure, which is positive for visiting cyclists. Expect to find plentiful cafés catering for cyclists, good local workshops and bike-hire facilities, and some of the finest roads you are ever likely to pedal over.

The Vuelta de España has passed through the region numerous times and in 2019 the steep road up to the Bernia Fort was completely resurfaced for when the Vuelta de Valencia used it as a stage finish. The climbs are often long, but usually gentle compared to gradients found in the UK, with around 6% average being fairly common.

Whenever driving on the mountain roads in this region, you may well mumble, "The Romans clearly didn't visit here". The twisting and switchback nature of the mountain roads can become a little tedious for the car driver, but as a cyclist this translates into pure pleasure, with turn after turn of silky-smooth tarmac.

All the following routes start in the village of Alcalalí in the Jalón/Xalo valley.

A note on temperatures: Although it will be tempting to set off without additional layers of warmer clothing, note that when in the shade and going downhill, it can feel surprisingly chilly. So pack a long-sleeve top, at least.

By law, all cyclists using public roads in Spain must wear a helmet and have a rear light. Although the police aren't known for stopping cyclists, it certainly can't be ruled out. And anyway, it is far safer to wear a helmet and have a rear light switched on.

Cycle hire
www.blancabikes.com, based in Jávea (Xàbia), offer cycle hire.

Grading
Routes in this section have been assigned the following grades:

- **Moderate:** Suitable for a reasonably fit novice. Some steep ascents and sections of technical descent. Up to 60km.
- **Difficult:** Longer climbs and steeper/longer descents with exposed sections. Up to 100km.
- **Very difficult:** Multiple long ascents with gradients reaching 20% at times. Technical descents involving hairpin bends on exposed sections of sometimes single-track road. Up to 130km.

ROUTE 57

Col de Rates, Tarbena and Castell de Castells

Start/finish	Alcalalí, ///earlobe.airlock.gusts
Distance	47km (84km with extension; 87km with both extensions)
Ascent	900m (1500m with extension; 1800m with both extensions)
Grade	Moderate (Difficult with extension)
Time	2hr 30min (4hr with extension; 4hr 30min with both extensions)

It's all about the climb up the Col de Rates, iconic as it is, and used by so many big teams on a daily basis. The average gradient up this is 5.5% and it is 7km to the top (350m ascent). There's a nice restaurant up there, too – so take a few euros for refreshments.

A fine, sweeping descent follows, before a short climb to Tarbena, then undulating tarmac with a wonderful mountain backdrop, all the way to Castell de Castells. The return leg is heavenly.

Access and parking

Easiest parking is opposite the Repsol fuel station on the outskirts of Alcalalí. If coming from the coast, turn off the N-332 onto the CV-750 and follow signs for Xaló/Jalón.

If you want to add a few extra kilometres to the ride, there is plentiful parking available in the towns of Jalón and Pedreguer, and the roads from either town to Alcalalí are excellent.

The ride

Before setting off, take note of Musette café at the road junction in Alcalalí. They have a workshop available for bikers and are super knowledgeable. The coffee is great too.

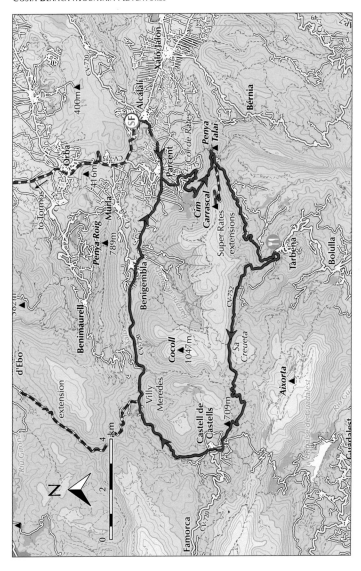

Take the CV-720 to **Parcent**. This passes through almond groves and provides a nice, gentle warm up. At the T-junction in Parcent go left onto the CV-715, signed for Tarbena. Here starts the famous climb of **Col de Rates**.

Now follows 7km of sublime hill-climbing of the highest quality. Never too steep, and with increasingly wonderful views across the Jalón valley, it's switchback after switchback as it wriggles up the side of the mountain.

Around 1km before the top, the going gets easier, but then comes a final assault on the leg muscles for a few hundred metres, before the crest and the 'finish line'. Pull in for the view at the very least. But better still, stop at the restaurant for a brew and one of their massive cakes.

Continue on the Tarbena road, with a truly epic mountain backdrop: the Ferrer and Bernia ridges are slightly to the left, and Puig Campana, Ponoch and Xanchet are straight ahead. This road was resurfaced in 2021 and is very smooth.

After a few kilometres of exhilarating descent comes more climbing, this time up to the outskirts of the mountain village of **Tarbena**. If wanting more refreshments, then ignore the right turning for Castell de Castells and go on for a few hundred metres to the village where there are a couple of cafés.

253

To continue with the route, turn right onto the **CV-752** towards Castell de Castells (Castle of the Castles) and follow this as it snakes through the mountain scenery, undulating but generally climbing, until the final section to **Puerto de Sa Creueta** weighs in at 12% – and feels it! (Looking up and rightwards to craggy ground you can see Cova del Dalt – Route 45.)

Now this may appear to be the top, but there is a little more climbing to do shortly, so be sure to keep something in the tank. After an initial descent, you will pass an abandoned hamlet followed by a short climb. Now comes the big descent. Hold on tight! This sweeping descent with the mighty Aixorta mountain towering over you to the left is simply magnificent and continues all the way to the mountain oasis of **Castell de Castells**.

At the road junction on the edge of the village, there are some benches and a covered seating area. Also, there is a water fountain where bottles can be refilled.

Go right at the junction, onto the **CV-720** towards Parcent and Pedreguer. The Hotel Serrella is just a few metres along here, offering hearty refreshments and cold drinks. A short climb to get out of the village leads to a wide and super-smooth road all the way back to Parcent.

It's a mild descent all the way, and can be a pleasant cruise or a superfast blast, depending on your mood. Now it's the rocky crest of Cavall Verd that provides the nobbly mountain scenery, and the road follows this all the way. Once in **Parcent**, retrace the route back to **Alcalalí**. Or, if you didn't manage all the cafés on round one, well, now's your chance to go again.

Extension

If this shorter route isn't enough, there's a natural extension that adds about 1.5 hours to the loop, if you decide to include it. See Route 58 for mapping.

After leaving Castell de Castells follow the **CV-720** until Villa Mercedes, and there turn left at a sign for Pla de Petracos. This single-track road – newly surfaced in 2019 – leads high up into the mountains, giving a feeling of wilderness. The first 4km rise gently through almond grooves. Then, as the road bears sharp right with big cliffs ahead, the gradient stiffens as it climbs the final 2km to the top. There is no sign to signify the high point, but you'll know, and the dramatic scenery will be reward enough. About 3.5km of mostly gentle descent leads to the hamlet of Vall d'Ebo. However, the final section does become steep, so test your brakes in advance! Turn right onto the CV-712 heading for Pego and straight away you'll embark on another fine 4km of climbing that leads up to Port d'Ebo. The maximum gradient is 9% and comes just before a series of switchbacks. There is a viewpoint part way up this road and it is worth stopping to take a look.

Just before you arrive at Port d'Ebo, you'll pass a donkey sanctuary where there are usually lots of donkeys, goats and birds. It's right beside the road (but they are fenced in). From the top, the coastal plain can be seen far below, and the next 7km of road offer probably the finest descent in the region, with switchback after switchback, big views and big drops. It is sublime. At the T-junction, turn right onto the **CV-715** towards Sagra, and just keep going – all the way back to Alcalalí. There is a short climb after you leave the village of **Orba** – so save some energy for that.

'Super Rates' extension

And if all that isn't enough, some locals will occasionally do the 'Super Rates'! This is a there-and-back extension, starting at the **Col de Rates**, and going all the way up to the Fire Lookout Station. It adds an additional 3km and 300m of climbing. Take heed of those numbers! The road goes across the restaurant car park and is unpaved for a few metres, but after this, the surface is reasonably okay. It is always very narrow, always steep with no barriers… and it provides some of the best views this region has to offer.

Add about 30 minutes for this extension.

ROUTE 58

Vall de Gallinera and Vall d'Ebo

Start/finish	Alcalalí, ///earlobe.airlock.gusts
Distance	85km (119km with extension)
Ascent	1450m (2100m with extension)
Grade	Difficult
Time	4hr (5hr 30min with extension)

This takes in two of the finest valleys in the region, both are a step back in time and offer grandeur and tranquillity in equal measure. By using the Vall de Gallinera to ascend, the gradient is gentler and more suited to those less familiar with long climbs. The scenery is magnificent throughout and, as a bonus, the route passes by many other routes, including: Segaria ridge (Route 4); Cresta del Migdia (Route 5); L'Atzúbia (Adsubia) crag (Route 35); Arista al Forat de la Forada (Route 10); and Barranco del Infierno (Routes 22 and 56). From the top of Vall de Gallinera look out for a prominent rocky ridge in the distance – this is Benicadell.

Access and parking

Easiest parking is opposite the Repsol fuel station on the outskirts of Alcalalí.
If coming from the coast, turn off the N-332 onto the CV-750 and follow
signs for Xaló/Jalón.

If you want to add a few extra kilometres to the ride, there is plentiful
parking available in the towns of Jalón and Pedreguer, and the roads from
either town to Alcalalí are excellent.

The ride

Take the CV-750 then **CV-715** towards Orba. This is a nice gentle start with some
fantastically distracting views over Parcent and the Jalón valley to take your mind
off cold muscles.

A fun descent leads into **Orba**. At the roundabout, turn right, staying on the
CV-715 towards Pego. The route passes through the small villages of **Tormos**

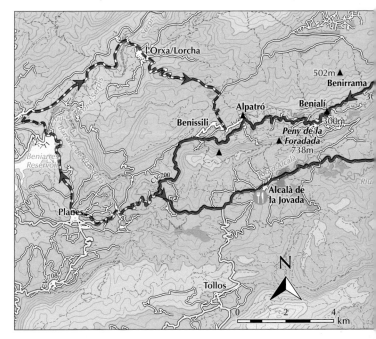

and **Sagra**, with the vast expanse of the Orba valley stretching towards the coast. During spring, orange blossom fills this valley with a wonderful aroma that can be fully appreciated on a bike. Beyond Sagra the road starts to climb, still fairly gently, but nonetheless you will feel a satisfying impression in your leg muscles. There are fine views of Segaria ridge (Route 4) and the big cliffs of Montgo in the distance. The Cresta del Migdia (Route 5), to your left, is closer.

On entering **Pego**, stay on the CV-715, initially following signs for Denia. This will lead to the **CV-700**, where you go left on this towards L'Atzúbia (Adsubia). There are many other ways to get through this town – with some being more direct, and arguably more of an adventure.

A long steady climb through the increasingly dramatic **Vall de Gallinera** lies ahead. As the road climbs, it takes you through seven pretty little villages, most offering refreshments. While ascending, look out for the big rock window high up on your left – this is the top of Route 10.

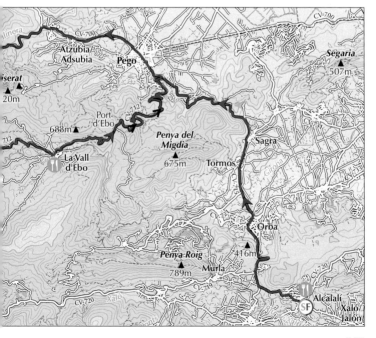

High above the Ebo valley

Some 25km and about 500m of climbing later, you will reach the top of the valley. Turn left here onto the **CV-712** towards Vall d'Ebo. More climbing soon follows but it's short-lived.

Alcalà de la Jovada is reached shortly after. The bar by the swimming pool has a nice terrace and serves good, simple food. At 48km this is just over halfway in terms of distance, but already about 870m of ascent is in the bag.

Stay on the CV-712, passing **Vall d'Ebo**, to reach the final significant climb of the day, Port d'Ebo. This has a maximum gradient of 9% and is about 4km.

The descent towards **Pego** is just fantastic. But take care, there are some big drops!

At the T-junction with CV-715, turn right and follow the outward route back to Alcalalí.

Lorcha extension

Note: This extension route is described in a clockwise direction due to the extremely steep climb that would be necessary if tackling it anti-clockwise. Apart from the first couple of kilometres of steep gradient, the route is similar in either direction. Allow an additional 1.5 hours for the extension, which adds around 34km and 650m of climbing.

The standard route detailed above is fantastic and will be more than enough for most people. However, for those wanting more climbing, and some of the quietest roads imaginable, here goes...

At the top of the **Vall de Gallinera**, continue on the CV-700 towards Planes, and shortly before this village turn right onto the **CV-711**, the tourist route of the **Beniarres Reservoir**. There are some lovely sweeping descents to reach the dam. Continue to the village of Beniarres, where there is a small, friendly bar. Skirt around the south and east of the village on the CV-705 to gain the CV-701 which follows the Serpis valley to **Lorcha**.

The road goes around the north and east side of Lorcha before a right turn by a warehouse marks the start of the next climb, which is about 5km and 350m of ascent at up to 11%. Thankfully it is a steady climb and offers superb views back to Lorcha and beyond. The road becomes undulating for the final couple of kilometres, then suddenly you reach a T-junction. Turn right here, and while you are on level terrain, take the opportunity to check your brakes – the next section gets a bit wild!

The road soon becomes single track, but it is super smooth. The descent into the Vall de Gallinera takes you to **Benissili**, but there are three hamlets all close to each other and arriving at any works just fine. But beware and stay focused: this descent is extremely steep with hairpins and steep drops.

Nearing the bottom of the descent you will reach the CV-714 is reached. Turn right onto this to re-join the **CV-700**, and continue with the standard route as described above.

 ROUTE 59

Bernia circuit

Start/finish	Alcalalí, ///earlobe.airlock.gusts
Distance	84km (95km with additional climb on south side)
Ascent	1450m (2100m with additional climb on south side)
Grade	Difficult
Time	3hr 45min (add 1hr if also climbing the south side from Altea la Vella)

This is the complete Bernia itinerary, providing top-quality road climbing on all sides of the mountain and always on fantastic surfaces.

It is also easy to split the route into sections, in case you don't want to go the full distance in one go. If you miss out the loop up to Port de Bernia you'll cut out 20km and a tough climb. Another way of reducing leg stress is to avoid the optional Vuelta-stage climb on the south side.

However this route is tackled, it is sure to be memorable, with ever-changing dramatic views of both mountain and coast.

Access and parking

Easiest parking is opposite the Repsol fuel station on the outskirts of Alcalalí. If coming from the coast, turn off the N-332 onto the CV-750 and follow signs for Xaló/Jalón.

If you want to add a few extra kilometres to the ride, there is plentiful parking available in the towns of Jalón and Pedreguer, and the roads from either town to Alcalalí are excellent.

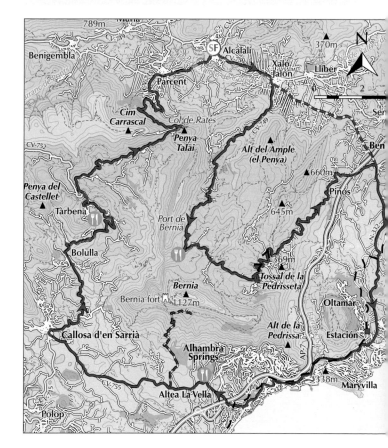

The ride

From Alcalalí follow the CV-750 to **Xaló/Jalón**, about 3km and all on the level. On entering the village, bear right at a mini roundabout by the supermarket, then follow the road as it turns sharp right, so as to skirt around the village. (A shortcut through the village – shown on the map – omits the climb over Port de Bernia and saves around an hour.)

Bear left on this road and, as it narrows to a single-track lane, look out for the welcoming doors of the Velosol Cycling Café – a good spot if you're in need of any spares, or a coffee.

Almost immediately after Velosol is a right turn onto the CV-749 with a sign for Bernia and Masserof. Turn onto this narrow lane, pass the police station on the left, and soon you leave the built-up area for the open road ahead.

This sinuous strip of tarmac now weaves a way through the Masserof valley at a maximum gradient of 8% and an average of around 5%. It is single track the whole way and is almost always very quiet – though expect more traffic at weekends and holiday times.

After 10km, **Port de Bernia** is reached. Make sure you look to the right for a mountain panorama that is hard to beat. But watch out, it is an easy one to miss because you have the massive Bernia ridge dominating the view straight ahead.

After Port de Bernia, the gradient flattens considerably and a few restaurants garnish the roadside. All are worthy of a stop and are very popular at weekends.

Stay on the **CV-749** as it bears left to begin the descent to **Pinós** and beyond. All in, this is about 16km, and it offers even more splendid scenery, with an increasingly coastal flavour.

Turn right onto the N-332 towards **Calpe**. This is the main coast road, but it is still relatively quiet much of the time as most traffic uses the nearby motorway. Stay on the **N-332** for 14km, passing through the dramatic Mascarat gorge as it descends on smooth surfaces.

Turn right onto the **CV-755** towards Callosa d'en Sarrià and Altea la Vella. Stay on this as you pass through **Altea la Vella**. Note that after the first mini-roundabout there is a water fountain on the right, so top up here if you need to. Continue towards **Callosa d'en Sarrià** – about 9km and undulating all the way.

At the mini-roundabout in Callosa, turn right towards Bolulla and the Fonts del Algar – this is well signposted. It's about 5km to

261

Mascarat gorge

Bolulla, with more undulating terrain and some finely sweeping bends to spice things up.

The mountains ahead hint of what is to come. Once through the little village of Bolulla, there follows a 7km climb with an average gradient of 5.5% and a maximum of 7.3% – so it's fairly steady. The landscape is quite 'Lord of the Rings' dramatic, with the Bernia massif to the right and the Bolulla canyons to the left.

The road skirts around the pretty mountain village of **Tarbena** and, just before the top of the climb, you reach the cyclists oasis of Pizza Bar Il Giro. You can get good coffee, cake and toasties here.

Once recharged, continue the short way to the top of the climb, with an easing of both the gradient and your worries. Seven kilometres of undulating mountain switchback, with the dramatic Sierra Ferrer to the right, leads to the **Col de Rates**. It's worth looking back from here to appreciate the stunning landscape you just came through.

An easy cruise through the mega-switchbacks of Col de Rates sees you into **Parcent**. Turn right here to roll back to **Alcalalí**. If it's not too late there could be cake on offer at Musette café, too.

Bernia south climb extension (the Vuelta-stage finish)

With its 5.5km of climbing, at an average of 12% and maximum of 24%, this will feel tough. It also adds 640m of ascent to the route, so only go for it if there's plenty left in your tank.

If you want to include this extension, turn off the Altea to Callosa road near Alhambra Springs, at a tourist sign for **Bernia Fort**. The road is single track the whole way, initially on a good surface and not steep. But don't get too used to the gradient – it changes ... a lot! Soon the surface improves markedly and is super smooth as it climbs at an increasingly lung-busting angle. The scenery is fabulous and helps to take the mind off this mighty undertaking. The final section is on concrete, but still smooth and pleasant enough. This is a 'there-and-back' extension, so when you're ready, head back down. But take care, as vehicles and other cyclists may be on their way up.

ROUTE 60
Serrella and Aitana circuit

Start/finish	Alcalalí, ///earlobe.airlock.gusts
Distance	128km
Ascent	2500m
Grade	Very difficult
Time	5hr 30min

This is a compelling route and a must for any cyclist who enjoys mountain roads and long, steady climbs. Most of the roads are quiet – only a short section through La Nucia bucks that trend. Once on the way to Finestrat, it's open road with the mighty Aitana mountain ahead. Our route completes a full circuit of the Aitaina and Serrella mountains. And it is not to be underestimated!

From the top of the Tudons Pass, a road leads off to the very summit of Aitana (1558m). But this land is owned by the military and closed to the public except for very special occasions – like, say, a visiting Vuelta de España.

Access and parking
Easiest parking is opposite the Repsol fuel station on the outskirts of Alcalalí. If coming from the coast, turn off the N-332 onto the CV-750 and follow signs for Xaló/Jalón.

If you want to add a few extra kilometres to the ride, there is plentiful parking available in the towns of Jalón and Pedreguer, and the roads from either town to Alcalalí are excellent.

Cerro de
les Cabanyes ▲

Pico
Patol ▲

Tossal de
la Creu ▲

Balones

Millena

Tollos

Benimassot

Facheca

Famorca

Gorga

Quatrondeta

Benilloba

CV-70

Benasau

Alcoleja

Confrides

Penàguila

CV-70

de
leta

Tudons Pass

Aitana ▲
1558m
125

Tudons
climb

Peñón
Divino ▲

de les
remanzanas

CV-782

Sella

Río Sello

El Castellet

Relleu

CV-758

CV-775

Orxeta

N

0   2   4
km

The ride

Before setting off, take note of Musette café at the road junction in Alcalalí. They have a workshop available for bikers and are super knowledgeable. The coffee is great too.

Take the CV-720 to **Parcent**. This passes through almond groves and provides a nice, gentle warm up. At the T-junction in Parcent go left onto the CV-715 and signed for Tarbena. And here starts the famous climb of **Col de Rates**.

Now follows 7km of sublime hill-climbing of the highest quality. Never too steep, and with increasingly wonderful views across the Jalón valley, it's switchback after switchback as it wriggles up the side of the mountain.

Around 1km before the top, the going gets easier, but then comes a final assault on the leg muscles for a few hundred metres, before the crest and the 'finish line'. Pull in for the view at the very least. But better still, stop at the restaurant for a brew and one of their massive cakes.

Continue on the Tarbena road, with a truly epic mountain backdrop: the Ferrer and Bernia ridges at slight to the left, and Puig Campana, Ponoch and Xanchet are straight ahead. This road was resurfaced in 2021 and is very smooth.

After a few kilometres of exhilarating descent comes more climbing, up to the outskirts of the mountain village of **Tarbena** where there are a couple of cafés.

The descent on the CV-715 to **Bolulla** and Callosa is wonderful, with loads of switchbacks and big mountain scenery for that all-important 'visual soundtrack'. Stay on the CV-715 through **Callosa**, where there are more places to stop for refreshments). Yet more fine descent lies in wait – as far as the Río Guadalest, and then a short ascent into **Polop**.

Go through Polop and join the busy CV-70 heading towards **La Nucia**, in the direction of Benidorm. The next 15 minutes or so is on fairly busy roads, though there is a cycle lane for part of the way.

Leave this busy thoroughfare when you reach the **CV-758** and go right towards Finestrat. This road is typically very quiet and in its latter stages you will get full-on views of the most iconic mountain in the region – the Puig Campana. Once seen, never forgotten.

In **Finestrat** there are refreshments for hungry cyclists and this is a pretty sensible place to arrange a break as it'll be a long time before you reach the next oasis.

Next, continue along the CV-758 towards Sella. Early on, there is a splendid descent on a road that seems far too wide for the almost non-existent traffic. Some steady climbing follows and soon you'll reach a T-junction. Turn right here, onto the **CV-770**, inland towards Sella. Look towards the right for fabulous views of the other faces of Puig Campana. Also note the 'sharks fin' of rock that is El Castellets – a ridge that is best completed over six days!

The road begins to climb and Sella will soon be seen ahead, nestling far below the summit of Aitana. Stay on this road as it winds its way through **Sella** and on to the beginning of the **Tudons Pass**. A signboard marks the start of this climb, but the road has already been climbing for many kilometres, so take the 11km as what's to come rather than what has been.

The road is never steep, but it is unrelenting as it gains almost 600m on the way to the 1025m high point.

Stay on the CV-770 to enjoy a scenic descent into Alcoleja, with an odd mix of abandoned military buildings and huge crags in juxtaposition.

Stay on the main road through the little village of **Alcoleja** – where there is a *font* (spring) with delicious water for recharging your bottles.

At the T-junction with the CV-70, go left towards Alcoy, and then soon turn right onto the CV-710 for **Gorga** (more refreshments available here).

If looking at a map of the area, it would appear that the CV-754 provides the most direct onward route, and it does. But, hiding along this narrow road, are some vicious ascents across deep ravines. So we recommend the more balanced option of taking the CV-720 going straight across the roundabout in Gorga and on to **Balones** and Benimassot.

As the road navigates around the edges of **Benimassot**, a few well-positioned benches appear. This is a good place to stop for a rest. Look towards the mountains to see the amazing limestone rock spires of the Serrella ranges.

From Benimassot, the road is fairly level to **Facheca**, where the descent begins, and goes on through **Famorca**, and on to **Castell de Castells**. The Serrella Hotel is another good refreshment stop.

Continue along the CV-720 as it gently descends all the way back to **Alcalalí**, through abundant almond and olive groves.

The long, glorious descent to the Jalón valley

APPENDIX A

Activity summary table

Ridges

	Route	Start	Grade (UIAA grade)	Total time (approach, route and descent)
1	Toix Ridge Integral (Este y Oeste)	Mirador above Maryvilla (Calpe)	IV	5hr 20min
2	Bernia Ridge	Bernia Restaurant / Casas de Bernia, CV-749, Jalón	IV	6–7hr
3	Sierra Ferrer Ridge	Casa Susi Restaurant, CV-749 (Bernia)	I	3hr 15min
4	Segaria Ridge	Segaria parking area, Partida Vinyals, Beniarbeig	IV+	10hr (full traverse); 5–6hr (Section 1); 3hr (Section 2); 4hr (Section 3)
5	Cresta del Migdia	Tormos cemetery	II	4hr
6	El Realet/Alt del Castellet	CV-758 between Finestrat and Sella	IV+	6hr 25min
7	Cresta del Canelobre, Cabezón de Oro	Cueves de Canelobre, Busot	III	2hr 20min
8	Forada Ridge	Xorret de Cati; Elda/Petrer	IV	3hr 45min
9	Benicadell Ridge	Casa de les Planisses, Beniatjar	IV+	7hr 30min
10	Arista al Forat de la Forada	Benissivi	IV+	4hr 40min
11	Cresta dels Bardals, Serrella	Casa Polselli; Port de Confrides, Confrides	IV+	3hr 40min

	Route	Start	Grade (UIAA grade)	Total time (approach, route and descent)
12	Cresta del Castellar	Calle de la Serreta, Alcoy	4+*	2hr 35min
13	Cresta del Maigmó	CV-805, near Agost	IV	3hr

* This route has been given a French grade because it is fully bolted.

Via ferratas

	Route	Start	Grade (Hüsler scale)	Total time (approach, route and descent)
14	Penya del Figueret	Penya del Figueret, Relleu	K2	2hr 30min
15	Ponoch (Ponoig)	Calle Camino del Flare, La Nucia	K4 (optional grade 2/3 scramble)	3hr 30min; 5hr 30min (including scramble)
16	El Cid	Road head, Casica del Forestal, Elda/Petrer	K4	3hr 40min
17	Redován	Swimming pool, Calle del Seminarista Ballesta, Redován	K2 (initial section); K5 (upper section)	3hr 15min (1hr 30min for lower section only)
18	Callosa de Segura	Cueva Ahumada recreation area, Callosa de Segura	K3 (first section); K5 (second section)	3hr 30min
19	Castillo Savatierra	Las Cruces recreation area, Villena	K2	2hr
20	Aventador	Near Alboi, Genovés	K3	1hr

Canyons

	Route	Start	Grade	Total time (approach, route and descent)
21	Barranco del Pas de Tancat	CV-715 Bolulla to Tarbena road, Bolulla	V4	4hr 20min
22	Barranco del Infierno	Fleix, Vall de Laguar	V4	6hr
23	Barranco dels Llidoners and de Racons	Benimaurell, Vall de Laguar	V5	5hr 10min
24	Barranco del Pas de Calvo	Pla de Petracos, Castell de Castells	V3	2hr 30min
25	Barranco de Parent	Alhama Springs, Altea la Vella	V4	3hr 40min
26	Barranco de l'Estret de Cardos	Pinós, Bernia	V3	3hr
27	Barranco de Mascarat	N-332 Mascarat tunnels, Calpe	V3	1hr 35min
28	Barranco del Curt o Pas de Bandolers	Port de Bernia, CV-749, Jalón	V4	5hr

Sport climbing

	Route	Location	Grade range (French system)
29	Alcalalí	Alcalalí	3+ to 6a+
30	Los Cerezos	Off CV-752 between Tarbena and Castell de Castells	4+ to 6b
31	Sierra de Toix	Road end beyond Castellet de Calpe, Calpe	3+ to 5
32	Candelabra del Sol	Road end beyond Castellet de Calpe, Calpe	5, 6a+, 6a+
33	Morro Falquí	Calle Fresnos, Benitaxell	5+ (6a+), 6a, 6c
34	Ambolo	Calle de la Torre Ambolo, near Cap de la Nau, Jávea	4+ to 6a
35	L'Atzúbia/Adsubia	CV-717 beyond Adsubia	5 to 6c
36	Sector Cuevas, Cabezón de Oro	Cueves de Canelobre, Busot	4+ to 6a+

Trad climbing

	Route	Location	Grade (UIAA system/ British system)	Total time (approach, route and descent)
37	Aristotles and Pepsi Crest, Puig Campana	Helipad beyond Font d' Moli, Finestrat	V+ (VS/HS)	7hr
38	Espolón Central, Puig Campana	Helipad beyond Font d' Moli, Finestrat	V- (HS)	8hr 10min
39	The Edwards Finish, Puig Campana	Font d' Moli, Finestrat	V- (VS)	7hr 30min
40	Via Gene, Cabezón de Oro	Cuevas de Canelobre, Busot	V (VS)	6hr 30min
41	Arista Agullo, Cabezón de Oro	Cuevas de Canelobre, Busot	IV+ (S/HS)	5hr 10min
42	Via Esther and Scorpion, Vall de Gulabdar	Vall de Gulabdar, Polop	IV+ & V (HS/VS)	2hr 30min–3hr & 2hr 30min–3hr
43	Via Pany, El Peñón de Ifach	Calpe marina	V (VS)	5hr 25min

Hikes

	Route	Start/finish	Distance	Ascent	Grade	Time
44	Mallada del Llop and El Regall	El Castellet recreation area, Castell de Castells	14km	1000m	Difficult	5hr
45	Cova del Dalt and Es Crestall	Puerto de Sa Creueta, Castell de Castells	7km	250m	Easy	2hr 30min–3hr
46	Xanchet circuit	Viewpoint at top of Vall de Gulabdar, Polop	14km	600m	Moderate	4hr 30min
47	Bernia Circuit and fort	Casas de Bernia, CV-749 road end	9.5km	350m	Moderate	4hr

Trail runs

	Route	Start/finish	Distance	Ascent	Grade	Time
48	Castell d'Axia	Llosa de Camacho	14km	650m	Moderate	2–3hr
49	Aixorta and Les Arcs	Les Arcs parking area, CV-752, Castell de Castells	15km	625m	Difficult	2hr
50	Corral de la Llacuna	CV-720 Benigembla to Castell de Castells road	12km	500m	Moderate	1hr 30min
51	Les Arcs and Raco Roig	Les Arcs parking area, CV-752, Castell de Castells	11km	350m	Moderate	1hr 20min
52	Castell de Granadella	Hipica riding school, Cumbre del Sol, Benitachell	7.5km	300m	Moderate	1hr 20min
53	Sierra de Olta	Zona d'Acampada, Olta/Calpe	12km	450m	Moderate	1hr 45min
54	Puig Campana	Bridge beyond Font de Molí, Finestrat	15.5km	1070m	Difficult	3hr
55	Penya Gros and Forada	Alcalà de la Jovada	11km	300m	Moderate	1hr 40min
56	Barranco del Inñerno circuit	Fleix, Vall de Laguar	13km	800m	Difficult	2hr 30min

Road cycling

	Route	Start/finish	Distance	Ascent	Grade	Time
57	Col de Rates, Tarbena and Castell de Castells	Alcalí	47km (84km with extension)	900m (1500m with extension)	Moderate (Difficult with extension)	2hr 30min (4hr with extension)
58	Vall de Gallinera and Vall d'Ebo	Alcalí	85km (119km with extension)	1450m (2100m with extension)	Difficult	4hr (5hr 30min with extension)
59	Bernia circuit	Alcalí	84km (95km with extension)	1450m (2100m with extension)	Difficult	3hr 45min (4hr 45min with extension)
60	Serrella and Aitana circuit	Alcalí	128km	2500m	Very difficult	5hr 30min

APPENDIX B
Useful contacts

Local information
www.mountain-journeys.co.uk is the author's website where an up-to-date blog is maintained and many activities are available. We have offered guiding services in the region for many years, so do get in touch if you'd like some help

Accommodation and guiding
http://theorangehouse.co.uk
www.compasswest.co.uk

Public transport
www.renfe.com/es/en For up-to-date information on train services
www.alsa.com/en/web/bus/home For bus service information
www.beniconnect.com For airport shuttle services

Insurance
www.thebmc.co.uk/insurance
www.snowcard.co.uk
www.truetraveller.com

Shops
Decathlon, www.decathlon.es, have large shops in Alicante, Benidorm, Gandía, and Ondara. All sell climbing and hiking equipment.
La Gruta, www.egruta.com, is a climbing shop in the town of La Nucia, near Finestrat.
Librería Europa, www.libreria-europa-calpe.com, in Calpe, stocks a wide range of English-language books, including outdoor texts.

Cycle hire and repair
Blanca Bikes, www.blancabikes.com, based in Jávea, offer cycle hire.
Bicicletas Boronat, www.bicicletesboronat.com, based in Gata de Gorgos, is the place for all mechanical repairs.

Weather forecasts
www.aemet.es/en/portada

Emergencies
The European emergency number is 112.

APPENDIX C
Castilian – Valencian – English glossary

Castellano	Valenciano	English
abejas	abelles	bees
anidación de aves	anidació d'ocells	bird nesting (restrictions)
animales salvajes	animals salvatges	wild animals
area recreativa	area recreativa	picnic area
autopista	autopista	motorway
autovía	autovia	dual carridgeway
avispas	vespes	wasps
barranco	barranc	gorge/canyon
bomberos forestales	bombers forestalls	fire lookout station
cabras salvajes	cabres salvatges	wild goats
camino	camí	track
camino privado	camí privat	private driveway
capilla	capella	chapel
carretera	carretera	road
casa	casa	house
casita	caseta	small house/cottage
castillo	castell	castle
cumbre	cim	summit
colina	turo	hill
collado	coll / pujol	pass
coto de caza	coto de caça	hunting area
cresta	cresta	ridge
cruz	creu	cross
deposito de agua	deposit d'aigua	water tank
embalse	embassament	reservoir

Castellano	Valenciano	English
ermita – monasterio	ermita – monestir	hermitage
finca	finca	land/country property
fuente	font	well/spring
fuerte pendiente	fort pendent	steep road/terrain
fuertes corrientes	forts corrents	strong currents
GR (gran recorrido)	GR (gran recorregut)	long route
hoyo	forat	hole
jabalí	porc senglar	wild boar
lago	llac	lake
lavadero	llavador – safareig	wash-house
llano	plà	terrace/plain
mirador	mirador	viewpoint
montaña	muntanya	mountain
nevera	nevera	snowpit
peligro/riesgo de desprendimiento	perill de despreniment	danger/risk of rock slide
peña	penya	cliff/rocky bluff
perro peligroso	gos perillós	dangerous dog
pista	camí	track
playa	platja	beach
PR (pequeño recorrido)	PR (petit recorregut)	short route
privado (propiedad privada)	privado (propietat privada)	private (private property)
prohibido el paso	prohibit el pas	no trespassing
puente	pont	bridge
rapel	ràpel	abseil
riadas	riuades	flash floods
riesgo eléctrico	risc elèctric	electric danger
río	riu	river

Castellano	Valenciano	English
roca	roca	rock
ruta	ruta	itinerary
sendero/senda	sender/senda	footpath
sierra	serra	mountain range
simas	avenc	pothole/cave
terrenos irregulares	terrenys irregulars	uneven ground/terrain
torre	torre	tower
valle	vall	valley
vía pecuaria	via pecuària	cattle (way) crossing

APPENDIX D
Further reading

Chris Craggs and Alan James, *Rockfax – Costa Blanca*. An informative and up-to-date guidebook, mostly containing sport-climbing crags, but some trad is there too.

Joan Crespo Sempere, *Crestas y Aristas de la Comunidad Valenciana*. By a local climber, this details 23 ridges throughout the region and is in Spanish.

Terry Fletcher, *Walking on the Costa Blanca* (published by Cicerone). If searching for more walking routes, this is a good place to start.

APPENDIX E

Climbing grades comparison table

CLIMBNG GRADE COMPARISONS			
UK TRAD	UK TECH	FRENCH SPORT GRADE	UIAA
M	3a	1	I
		2	II
D	3b	2+	III
		3-	III+
VD	3c	3	IV-
S	4a	3+	IV
		4a	IV+
HS	4b	4b	V-
VS		4c	V
	4c	5a	V+
HVS		5b	VI-
	5a	5c	VI
E1		6a	VI+
	5b		
E2		6a+	VII-
	5c		
E3		6b	VII
		6b+	
E4	6a	6c	VII+

NOTES